JAN KAPLAN, is an award-winn[...] and a notable Prague histori[...] since 1968. He has co-autho[...] *Prague in the Shadow of the Swastika*, *Prague, The Turbulent Century* and *Prague 1900–2000*. Among his many documentary film productions, he has co-directed the Channel 4 series *In Search of Holy England* and *The Assassination of Reinhard Heydrich* shown on BBC Timewatch.

A TRAVELLER'S COMPANION TO

PRAGUE

EDITED BY

Jan Kaplan

ROBINSON
London

While every effort has been made to trace the owners of copyright material reproduced herein, the publishers would like to apologize for any omissions and will be pleased to incorporate missing acknowledgements in any future editions.

Constable & Robinson Ltd
3 The Lanchesters
162 Fulham Palace Road
London W6 9ER
www.constablerobinson.com

First published in the UK by Robinson,
an imprint of Constable & Robinson Ltd 2005

A copy of the British Library Cataloguing in
Publication Data is available from the British Library.

ISBN 1-84529-074-7

Printed and bound in the EU

1 3 5 7 9 10 8 6 4 2

To Ela, Marynia and Waldek

Contents

CHARACTER OF A CITY

PRAGUE

EARLY BEGINNINGS

FIRST IMPRESSIONS

THE CASTLE AND HRADČANY

THE LEGEND OF ST WENCESLAS

ST VITUS' CATHEDRAL

THE OLD ROYAL PALACE

THE GOLDEN LANE

THE ROYAL SUMMER PALACE

THE ČERNÍN PALACE

THE WALLENSTEIN PALACE

THE FORMER ROTHES HAUS AND THE SHÖNBORN PALACE

THE CHARLES BRIDGE AND THE VLTAVA

THE OLD TOWN

JOSEFOV

THE OLD PRAGUE GHETTO

PRAGUE LIFE, CUSTOMS, MORALS

EATING AND DRINKING

SEX IN BOHEMIA

Illustrations

All pictures courtesy of the Kaplan Productions Archive

Plates

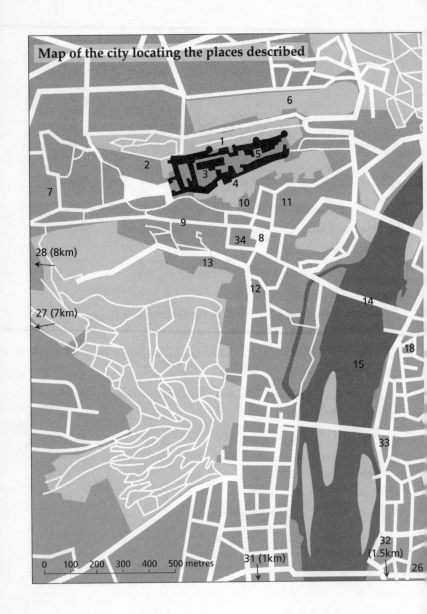

Map of the city locating the places described

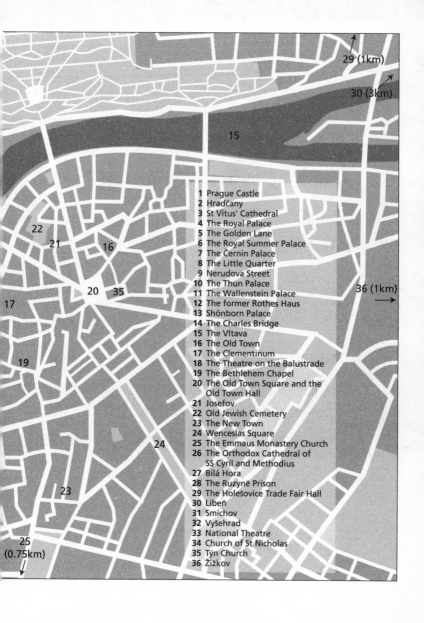

29 (1km)

30 (3km)

15

36 (1km)

1 Prague Castle
2 Hradčany
3 St Vítus' Cathedral
4 The Royal Palace
5 The Golden Lane
6 The Royal Summer Palace
7 The Černin Palace
8 The Little Quarter
9 Nerudova Street
10 The Thun Palace
11 The Wallenstein Palace
12 The former Rothes Haus
13 Shönborn Palace
14 The Charles Bridge
15 The Vltava
16 The Old Town
17 The Clementinum
18 The Theatre on the Balustrade
19 The Bethlehem Chapel
20 The Old Town Square and the
Old Town Hall
21 Josefov
22 Old Jewish Cemetery
23 The New Town
24 Wenceslas Square
25 The Emmaus Monastery Church
26 The Orthodox Cathedral of
SS Cyril and Methodius
27 Bilá Hora
28 The Ruzyně Prison
29 The Holešovice Trade Fair Hall
30 Liben
31 Smíchov
32 Vyšehrad
33 National Theatre
34 Church of St Nicholas
35 Týn Church
36 Žižkov

25
(0.75km)

Acknowledgements

I am extremely grateful to all the people who have helped me to collect material for this book. I should like to single out the following for help of various kinds:

Vlasta Gyenes, Martin Heller, Jana Hollanová, Kateřina Kostarová, Ivan Margolius, Devana Pavlíková, Martin Petiška.

My thanks above all to my wife Krystyna for invaluable support, both literary and domestic.

Rulers of Bohemia

DUKES OF BOHEMIA

Bořivoj	?-889 (?)
Spytihněv I	?-915(?)
Vratislav I	915(?)-921(?)
Václav (Wenceslas)	?-935
Boleslav I	935-(967/972-999)
Boleslav II	967/972-999
Boleslav III	999-1002
Vladivoj	1002-1003
Boleslav III	1003
Jaromír	1003
Boleslav Chrabrý (B. the Brave)	1003-1004
Jaromír	1004-1012
Oldřich	1012-1033
Jaromír	1033-1034
Oldřich	1034
Břetislav I	1035-1055
Spytihněv II	1055-1061
Vratislav II	1061-1092

Konrád I	1092
Břetislav II	1092–1100
Bořivoj II	1101–1107
Svatopluk	1107–1109
Vladislav I	1109–1117
Bořivoj II	1117–1120
Vladislav I	1120–1125
Soběslav I	1125–1140
Vladislav II	1140–1172
Bedřich	1172–1173
Soběslav II	1173–1178
Bedřich	1178–1189
Konrád II Ota	1189–1191
Václav II	1191–1192
Přemysl I	1192–1193
Jindřich Břetislav	1193–1197
Vladislav Jindřich	1197

KINGS OF BOHEMIA

Přemysl I	1198–1230
Václav I	1230–1253
Přemysl II Otakar	1253–1278
Václav II	1278–1305
Václav III	1305–1306
Jindřich Korutanský	1306
Rudolf I (Habsburg)	1306–1307
Jindřich Korutanský	1307–1310
Jan Lucemburský (John of Luxenbourg)	1310–1346
Karel IV (Charles IV)	1346–1378
Václav IV (Wenceslas IV)	1378–1419
The Hussite Wars	1419–1434
Zikmund (Sigismund of Luxenbourg)	(1420) 1436–1437
Albrecht II (Habsburg)	1437–1439

Ladislav Pohrobek (L. the Posthumous)	1453–1457
Jiří z Poděbrad (George of Podřbrad)	1458–1471
Ladislas II Jagiello	1471–1516
Ludvík Jagiello	1516–1526
Ferdinand I (of Habsburg)	1526–1564
Maxmilián II	1564–1576
Rudolf II	1576–1611
Matthias	1611–1619
Ferdinand II	1619
Frederick (Elector Palantine)	1619–1620
Ferdinand II	1620–1637
Ferdinand III	1637–1657
Leopold I	1657–1705
Joseph I	1705–1711
Charles VI	1711–1740
Maria Theresa	1740–1780
Charles Albert (as Czech king Charles III)	1741–1743
Joseph II	1780–1790
Leopold II	1790–1792
Francis II	1792–1835
Ferdinand V	1835–1848
Franz Joseph I	1848–1916
Charles I	1916–1918

Czech and Czechoslovak Presidents

Tomáš Garrigue Masaryk	1918–1935
Edvard Beneš	1935–1938
Emil Hácha	1938–1939
The German Occupation	1939–1945 (The 'State President' Emil Hácha)
Edvard Beneš	1945–1948
Klement Gottwald	1948–1953
Antonín Zápotocký	1953–1957
Antonín Novotný	1957–1968
Ludvík Svoboda	1968–1975
Gustáv Husák	1975–1989
Václav Havel	1989–1992
Václav Havel	1993–2003 (The Pres. of the Czech Republic)
Václav Klaus	2003–

Introduction

On 14 March 1939 the President of Czechoslovakia Emil Hácha was summoned by Hitler to Berlin. At 1 a.m. on the 15 March, Hácha was ushered into the presence of Hitler who warned him that the German Army was ready to invade Czechoslovakia. Hitler demanded surrender. Unless the president signed a paper requesting Hitler to take the Czech people under the protection of the Reich, hundreds of bombers would reduce Prague to ashes within a few hours. The elderly, sick Hácha fainted and had to be revived with an injection of dextrose and vitamins. Worn out by the bullying and blackmail he capitulated and signed the document. Prague, one of the most enchanting cities in Europe with a history of over a thousand years was saved. But she could have easily met the fate of Warsaw.

The city's ancient history and the lives of her princes are connected to two seats of power situated on two hills; the Hradčany with its splendid Castle and Vyšehrad embedded on the other side of the River Vltava. Everywhere around was a forest, 'melodious with buzzing swarms of bees and the songs of diverse birds. The beasts of the forest were beyond counting, like sand on the sea-shore or the stars in heaven . . .' In this paradise the legendary Princess Libuše, while standing on the rock of Vyšehrad, pointed to the site of Hradčany as the best place to build the Castle and, displaying her great powers of divination, foretold the future greatness of Prague with the words that every Czech child knows by heart, 'I see a town, the glory of which will reach the stars.' Libuše married a man who was found by her consorts constructing a threshold (*práh*) of a house. Although his original profession was that of a ploughman, he seemed a natural born ruler. They married, beginning the dynasty of Přemyslid which ruled the country until the beginning of the fourteenth century.

The first known traveller's description of Prague dates from c.965, when Ibrahim-Ibn-Jakub, a Moorish Jew from Tortosa in Spain who accompanied the Khalif of Cordoba on an embassy to central Europe, visited the great commercial town of stone-built houses. He commented with admiration on the town's wealth derived from commerce, the bustling trade in slaves, pelts, wheat, flour, horses, tin, gold and silver; on paying with linen banknotes and other curiosities such as the people's swarthy complexion and black hair. His observations of Slav women point to a lack of guilt in matters concerning sex: 'When a girl falls in love with some man or other, she will go to him and quench her lust.'

The Přemyslid rulers drew on the heritage of the Great Moravian Empire which thrived in the ninth century. Their defining cultural moment was the acceptance of Christianity which was introduced by two Greeks who translated liturgical texts into a language which we call the Old Church Slavonic. It was the works of these two saints, Cyril and Methodius, that introduced Christianity to a wide range of people. The new faith put an end to the slave trade and Prague soon acquired a saint of her own, the young Prince Václav (Wenceslas) whose ideals of right and justice brought him a martyr's death in c.930. He became the first great national saint whose importance can be seen in the exquisite beauty of the St Wenceslas Chapel in St Vitus' Cathedral, which was constructed above the saint's last resting place. The murals on the upper part of the chapel depict the legend of the life of St Wenceslas, while those on the lower level depict the suffering of Christ. Both levels are decorated with semi-precious stones set in gold mortar; some of the finest specimens of amethyst, jasper, agate, cornelian and chalcedony glow discreetly, enhancing the almost oriental splendour of the interior. Behind the metal-clad door of the chapel the Czech Crown Jewels are kept and only on a few important historical occasions can they be seen by the general public. For the Czechs this shrine is considered the 'holy of holies'.

So it is here in St Vitus' Cathedral that our Prague tour should begin. The cathedral, Prague's largest church, was founded 1344. The Romanesque basilica was pulled down and the King appointed Matthieu d'Arras was appointed in charge of the grand rebuilding. In the basement close to the royal crypt can be seen the excavated remains of the Romanesque St Vitus' Chapel. It was the arm of the saint which was brought as a holy relic from Saxony that upgraded the shrine to its higher status. From earliest times the Cathedral housed the tombs of Czech princes and kings and over the centuries it has become the nation's largest depository of works of art. Inside are paintings and sculptures, stained glass windows designed by outstanding painters, as well as objects kept in the treasury made of precious metals and stones, ivory and pearls.

Outside, on the south side of the Cathedral is a work created in the Gothic period: the Mosaic of the Last Judgement. It surmounts the arches of the 'Golden Gate' and is unique in artistic and technical terms. The mosaic was executed in sixty different shades of Czech glass by Venetian masters in 1370. The wealth of the Bohemian kingdom which is apparent in the St Wenceslas Chapel and the Mosaic of the Last Judgement was praised by many travellers. Bohemia, 'is rich in mines, and here are found a greater quantity of Agates and Topazes than in any other part of the world, as also Emeralds . . . This Country is more especially famous for its Mines of Copper, Iron, Silver and Gold,' wrote the Frenchman Charles Patin in 1695.

Taking a walk around the Castle's courtyards it is possible to imagine how the original castle was built and destroyed and re-built many times over. 'The Prague Castle had been plundered, devastated and deserted in as much as since the times of King Otakar II, that it had collapsed to the ground,' wrote Charles IV. From a humble dwelling of a pagan prince surrounded by a cluster of wooden dwellings, over the centuries this hilltop stronghold was transformed into a massive, royal palace. The South Wing where the president's offices are based, overlooks the third courtyard where stands a copy of the 1373 statue of St George. Known as the New Palace, it was designed by Nicolo Paccasi, the court architect of Empress Maria Theresa. In the second half of the eighteenth century Pacassi transformed the fortified castle into a habitable mansion in the Classical style. At this time the Habsburg emperors ruled from Vienna and only came to Prague for coronations. Towards the end of the eighteenth century Maria Theresa's successor Joseph II decided to use the ancient Castle as an artillery barracks. Many paintings, sculptures and other 'useless' objects were removed and sold at an auction in order to make room for ammunition.

Next to the New Palace stands a much older structure, built in the second half of the fifteenth century. This is the Old Palace with its supremely elegant Vladislav Hall, which is built in the Late Gothic style and reveals elements of Renaissance architecture. It is named after Vladislav Jagiellon, the son of the King of Poland, who was offered the throne after the death of the last Bohemian king, George of Poděbrady, in 1471. Vladislav's reign was threatened on a number of occasions by George's scheming son-in-law, the Hungarian Matthias, who not only attempted to get hold of the Bohemian royal regalia but also hired a poisoner to kill King Vladislav. The magnificent Hall was used for coronations of Bohemia's kings and for banquets. The Imperial Diet assembled here, for paying homage, for conferring knighthoods and for jousting tournaments. The knights would enter the Hall via the rider's staircase on their horses, the man and the beast adorned with coats of arms, ready to perform for the king and a crowd of excited nobles.

Here on Hradčany hill history has been made by various rulers. This was the original seat of the Přemyslid dynasty. When Prague was made a bishopric in 973 its status was elevated to that of other independent Christian centres in the West. For a brief period the seat of power was moved across the river to Vyšehrad by Count Vratislav II, who in 1085 became the first Czech king. Sixty-five years later it was moved back to Hradčany. The whole area to the west of the Castle grew and in the early thirteenth century the district of Hradčany was founded.

Just below the Castle another township, later to be called the Little Quarter, was established in 1257. The merchants who thrived there were mostly German colonists who traded with the settlement on the right bank of Vltava, which was the meeting place of several trade routes. The river, like an eight-lane highway brought most of the traffic. In the year 1090 the chronicler Cosmas enthused, 'Nowhere have you a better opportunity of enriching yourself, nowhere can you increase your position and fortune more than under the castle walls of Prague and in the Vyšehrad Street. There you will find Jews with the greatest abundance of gold and silver, there the wealthiest merchants of every nation, there the richest bankers, there markets where great bargains can be made . . .' Jewish merchants, traders from Germanic and Latin countries settled in the so-called *týn*, or courtyard, where at a later date the Gothic church of the Virgin Mary raised aloft its graceful spires. Týn (which is today called the Old Town) formed a separate township and was granted a municipal charter in around 1230.

As we walk towards St George's Square and pass the oldest part of the Cathedral with its notched spires, ogee windows and sneering gargoyles – the part which was built during the reign of Charles IV – it cannot but help bring to mind the work of this exceptional ruler who had the greatest impact on Prague by spotting original talent and by supporting it generously. Charles displayed an astute grasp of politics by managing to preserve peace for a long period allowing Prague to prosper. He inherited the Přemyslid genes from his mother Eliška and those of his father John of Luxemburg, a true knight-errant who died in France at the battle of Crécy in 1346. Charles was French-educated and became the King of Bohemia and Holy Roman Emperor after his father's death. During his reign (1346–78) Prague's panorama was altered and the city enlarged considerably. Peter Parler, the second architect of St Vitus' Cathedral, was also responsible for the construction of the bridge which still stands today and which is named after Charles. Prague attracted scholars and artists from all over Europe during this period. Men like the Italian poet Petrarch who criticised Charles' love of Prague: 'That country, which thou callest thy homeland, thy homeland was, but it ceased to be from that moment when thou becomest emperor.'

Many Germans agreed with Petrarch, jealous that Charles made Prague the centre of the Holy Roman Empire and showered her with riches and affection. The city also prospered by becoming an archbishopric in 1344. Already the Little Quarter and the Old Town, which in those days were enclosed by walls, were bursting with an ever-growing population. Charles therefore decided on building a new city on the right bank of the Vltava. The chronicler, Beneš of Weitmil tells us that, 'in the year of the Lord MCCCXLVIII, on the day of St Marc, our Lord Charles, King of the Romans and of Bohemia, laid the first stone, and founded the new city of Prague, building a very strong wall with ramparts and high towers extending from the Castle of Vyšehrad to Poříč. The Vyšehrad Hill also he surrounded with a wall and very strong towers, and the whole work was carried out within two years. And he also ordered that gardens and vineyards should be planted around the city of Prague.'

The New Town incorporated the former horse and cattle markets (the Wenceslas and Charles Squares). In the same year, 1348, Charles founded the university, so that, 'our loyal subjects in this kingdom, who have ceaselessly hungered for the fruits of knowledge, should not have to beg for alms in foreign lands.' It was the first university in Central Europe. Sixteen miles outside Prague another magnificent castle was erected where Charles spent time devising new projects. Karlštejn became a safe sanctuary for the new crown jewels, including the St Wenceslas crown which on Charles' orders was copied from the Přemyslid original. After his reign, the crown came to adorn the heads of another twenty-one kings and queens of Bohemia.

In 1380 the plague ravaged Prague and famine threatened the country's economic system. 'Tormented mothers eat their children and wolves attack even people who are armed with crossbows, and devour those they kill,' reported the fifteenth-century chronicle of Jan Długosz. Długosz knew Bohemia's problems quite well and visited Prague after one of his pupils, Vladislav Jagiellon was crowned king. Fearful people predicted the end of the world, but when it did not come the intensity of life among the Prague inhabitants was enhanced. This new mood of optimism in the city was captured succinctly by a university teacher and later archbishop of Prague, who said, 'The one good beverage is wine, the one good repast is meat and the one joy a woman.'

There was one man, however, who was determined to put an end to the clergy's 'good repast', as well as the sale of indulgences, the greedy acquisition of land, and the conduct of services in Latin. Jan Hus (c.1372–1415) sometime rector of the University at Prague, a man who was inspired by the writings of the Englishman John Wyclif, gave sermons in the Czech language at the Bethlehem Chapel and demanded reforms of the Church. This pioneer became a focus of Czech resentment against the largely German hierarchy. Hus and the whole Czech nation were excommunicated. He appealed to a General Council of the Church. Promised safe conduct he travelled to Constance for a meeting of the Council, but instead he was arrested and burned at the stake.

The Czechs were outraged by this betrayal and following a provocation by the Catholics, in 1419 they attacked the New Town Hall and threw their Catholic town councillors out of the window in the first ever Prague defenestration. The Pope responded by announcing a general crusade against the Hussite heretics. King Sigismund of Hungary and an army of 30,000 attacked the 'Czech heretics' who administered a crushing defeat to the crusaders. The Hussites were led by the fearless Jan Žižka, whose statue on a magnificent steed crowns the hill of Žižkov on the opposite side of Hradčany. Year after year, the Hussites were victorious against the invading foreign armies. They formulated a programme called the Four Articles of Prague in which they demanded freedom to preach and the administration of communion 'in both kinds' (i.e., not only 'the body of the Lord' – the Host – but the wine, 'the blood of the Lord' as well. Therefore the chalice became the symbol of the Hussites). The Hussite wars lasted from 1419 to 1434 and brought destruction to both the Castle and the city.

Before we leave the Castle area, just behind the Romanesque Basilica of St George and the Benedictine convent of which the first abbess, Princess Mlada, had a right to crown the queens of Bohemia, we should explore the Golden Lane. This short, narrow cul-de-sac, consisting of sixteen small houses is imbued with the myth of Emperor Rudolf's alchemists, although it was only the Castle guards and gold beaters who lived there. It was originally called Goldsmiths' Lane and dates back to the second half of the sixteenth century. The whole period of Emperor Rudolf II's reign (1576–1612) was one of the most extraordinary times in the history of the Castle. The Emperor assembled the most brilliant artists and scientists of the age. Inventions such as a pump, a musical automaton and hydraulic machines were made here. Alchemists working in utter secrecy searched frantically for the elixir of life and formulae for making gold. Clock makers, glass cutters, mineral experts, ivory, horn and amber carvers who excelled in glyptic art; embroiderers, draughtsmen, miniature and landscape painters, sculptors, landscape gardeners who planted the first tulip bulbs brought from Turkey; musicians and composers, mathematicians, philosophers and astronomers, men who talked to angels, spies and common con men, all mingled here at one time or another.

The melancholy Emperor would often take one of his lions for a walk. Whilst out he would check on those of his alchemists who had failed to deliver the elixir of life and been punished by imprisonment in cages left hanging from the trees lining the Castle alley. A paranoid and suspicious man constantly thinking of his brother Matthias who was plotting his fall, Rudolf, the 'great-grandson of the mad Juana of Castile', submerged himself in an obsessive collecting mania, as if the beautiful and strange objects he purchased were talismans; his secret keys to unknown worlds, worlds better than the one he knew. A part of Rudolf's priceless art collection including Giuseppe Arcimboldo's portraits composed using images of fruit and flowers, vegetables, roots, leaves and straw, were either removed by Rudolf's brother to Vienna, or plundered by the Saxons in 1632, or by the Swedes in 1648. One of the few pictures in Rudolf's collection still at Prague, Albrecht Dürer's *Madonna*, was purchased in Venice and carried 'by four stout men' across the Alps to Prague.

Rudolf was a man who understood art and foresaw the age of science. Although he was brought up to believe in the right of God to run the universe by miracle, he supported men of science who advanced the study of astronomy and alchemy (which evolved into chemistry and physics). Tycho Brahe, the Danish astronomer, was invited by the Emperor to work in Prague observing stars and planets, which he did with unprecedented accuracy after discovering serious errors in astronomical tables. Brahe rejected the Copernican theory, but his colleague Johannes Kepler showed this model to be essentially correct using Brahe's data. Kepler was appointed imperial astronomer in succession to Brahe and in his works proved that the paths of the planets are really elliptical (in the system of Copernicus the planets travel in circles). Kepler's laws of planetary motion formed the groundwork of Isaac Newton's discoveries in England.

After Rudolf's death in 1612 tensions began to mount inside the Empire. In 1618 a small group of Protestant leaders went to the Castle to request an audience. Following an exchange of insults the second Prague defenestration took place, with the Protestants throwing out three imperial representatives. Although all three survived the long fall, it signalled that the Czechs were in open revolt and it started the Thirty Years War. Between the battle of the White Mountain (now in the suburbs of Prague) in 1620 and the end of the Thirty Years War in 1648 the country was defiled by one army after the other. Prague lost its royal splendour and its Castle was left empty and mute, a relic of past glories. Since Rudolf's times the rulers of Bohemia, the Habsburgs, have inhabited the Castle very rarely, running their multinational realm from imperial Vienna. Bohemia lost her independence and her people were re-Catholicised and Germanized by the Austrians.

The White Mountain battle marked the end of ancient glory and the onset of a decline that was to last for 300 years. Although Prague became a mere provincial city on the peripheries of the Habsburg Empire, nevertheless foreign armies felt that it deserved to be attacked, as in the assault it suffered during the War of the Austrian Succession in 1741–8. The English historian Thomas Carlyle described how the Saxons, Bavarians and French took Prague in 1741 using an 'escalade' (imaginatively extending their short ladders with gallows to climb over the high walls of Vyšehrad). He also gave us an account of the Prussian siege which took place in 1757 during the Seven Years War. The army of Frederick the Great bombarded the city for several days. Prague was taken but eventually the Prussians were chased out by the Austrians. It was during this war that the Empress Maria Theresa lost the wealthy region of Silesia to the new European power – the Prussia of Frederick the Great.

My favourite panorama of Prague can be seen from the top of the Hradčany hill looking down on the city below. This is the view which was imprinted on the minds of Bohemia's rulers since it was here they lived and from where they governed; surrounded by their courtiers who erected houses on the steep slopes. After the collapse of the Austro-Hungarian Empire in 1918, the government of Tomáš

Masaryk of the newly independent Czechoslovakia also worked from here. When Hitler's armies invaded Czechoslovakia in 1939, the Nazis occupied most of the Castle buildings. Hitler himself came to the Castle in March 1939, had a Pilsner beer and from the second floor gazed down at his magnificent conquest.

After 1948 the Communists controlled this hill of power. In the proximity of power there is always a senseless violence and a well-concealed murder. In March 1948 not too far from the Hradčany Castle, outside the Černín Palace in Loretánské Square, the body of Foreign Minister Jan Masaryk (the son of Tomáš Masaryk) was found. He was murdered by the NKVD (the predecessor of the KGB) for being an outspoken critic of the Communists' methods of intimidation and their ruthless takeover of the country. Masaryk's death marked the end of democracy and the beginning of a regime which lasted till 1989. Sir Robert Lockhart, a British representative to the Czechoslovak Provisional Government befriended Jan Masaryk and in his diaries gave the most moving account of this man who probably by then already sensed that his death sentence had been issued by Moscow.

If you look down from Hradčany at the Little Quarter which is centred on the verdigris-covered cupola of the Baroque church of St Nicholas, there is much to admire in the combination of colours. What blends the different shapes from different architectural periods, is the *verdigris*, which translates poetically as the 'green of Greece', the dusty bluish-green patina that forms on copper, bronze and brass. The colour is offset by the rusty-brown tiles of the medieval roofs. The earthly hues and the pale green created by nature are aesthetically pleasing and complement each other in a gentle and harmonious way.

The Little Quarter burnt down completely in 1419 and suffered fire damage again in 1503 and 1541. After the battle on the White Mountain a wave of German migration swept over Prague taking possession of empty houses and seizing the trades and businesses that had been abandoned by Czech nobles and burghers. The imperial nobility and

Catholic clergy also moved in, erecting sumptuous palaces which today house government buildings and foreign embassies. Catholicism was recognized as the official religion and the new Baroque architecture came to epitomize the Habsburg rulers' faith.

The city's sublime plasticity makes her endlessly attractive regardless from which of the seven hills we examine her. Walking around *Praha*, as we call her in Czech, is like watching a good film. Images from a bird's eye view intercut with shots from street level and close-ups; it surprises us with its unexpected variety and there are so many slopes to look from, so many details to savour and so many different combinations to discover. Although I was born here I still find new details previously missed and I still marvel at the electric charge I get from the talent and energy which is trapped forever in the various sublime shapes that have been created by its architects and craftsmen.

I often stroll at a leisurely pace down Nerudova Street because it reminds me of an old custom of marking houses with painted signs, which started in the thirteenth century and continued until the eighteenth. In the past the look of Nerudova Street allowed me to travel back in time, far away from the Communist reality of my childhood. The street was named after the Czech journalist and writer Jan Neruda (1834–91) whose tales of the Little Quarter immortalized the bohemian lifestyle of the area. During one of his walks he discovered, to his astonishment, ten virgins living in the house of The Three Virgins. Subconsciously I keep checking the signs and the houses as I pass: The Two Suns, where Neruda lived, The Black Lion gripping a tankard between its paws, The Green Lobster, The White Beetroot which once belonged to someone who cultivated the market garden on Strahov; St Wenceslas on horseback identifies a former pharmacy, the Bretfeld Palace at No 33 where Casanova and Mozart attended balls, The Gold Wheel, The Gold Key, The Golden Crown Palace, Morzín Palace with its Baroque attention-grabbing facade, The Golden Goblet, the Golden Anchor and at No 12, The Three Violins where an instrument-making family once lived. According to Angelo Rippelino in his book *Magic Prague*, 'The charming sign of the Three Violins in Nerudova Street could easily stand as a symbol for the doleful music-making of Malá Strana'.

I follow the cobblestoned street until I arrive at St Nicholas' Church where Wolfgang Amadeus Mozart played on the organ during his stay in Prague in 1787. While Vienna and Salzburg did not take any notice of his death, Prague greatly lamented his passing. Over 4,000 people came to St Nicholas' to hear his friend sing a Requiem in his memory. 'There was a stupid rivalry, of which we find traces in the days of Mozart, between Vienna and Prague, and it was generally understood that whoever was applauded at Vienna was to be hissed at Prague, and *vice versa*'. That was how one critic explained the strange phenomenon of Prague's failure to appreciate Paganini. Whatever the justification, the truth is that the only community which recognized Mozart and showered him with the affection and the recognition for which he was starved elsewhere, was the one in Prague.

The city's *pièce de résistance* is the Charles Bridge which features slender Gothic gates at both ends. Its predecessor was built in 1158–72 and was the first stone bridge over the Vltava. King Vladislav I named it after his wife Judith. Pedestrians could cross the bridge without paying a toll, with the exception of Jews for whom the needs of trade compelled repeated crossings. They were obliged to pay two deniers each time. This Romanesque bridge was destroyed by floods in 1342. It took Peter Parler thirty-five years to finish the new bridge, which he did in 1390. It comprised sixteen arches and two new towers. The towers and the installation of the Baroque statues in the eighteenth century made the bridge one of the city's greatest attractions. The oldest statue on the bridge is that of Jan (or Johannes) Nepomuk, the canon of the Prague Cathedral Chapter who, according to a legend, was thrown into the river by the henchmen of the wicked King Wenceslas IV for refusing to reveal what the Queen had told him in the confessional. When in 1719 his tomb was opened a miraculous thing was noted, Nepomuk's tongue was red and fresh although his body had rotted. Ten years later he was canonized. The Saint's tongue, which refused to betray its vow of secrecy, was carried in a reliquary by the archbishop in a gala procession which ended with brilliant fireworks. Nepomuk supposedly performs miracles, very much like the Infant Jesus of Prague, the little wax statue of a toddler in the Church of Virgin Mary the Victorious in the Little Quarter. I keep reminding myself that Nepomuk replaced Jan Hus and I have seen a statue of a saint wearing a biretta with the five-starred halo round his head. The figure once represented Jan Hus and has been renamed as Nepomuk.

The graceful statues on the Charles Bridge remind me that after the battle on the White Mountain the Austrians re-Catholicised the Czechs, that 300,000 were forced to emigrate and that their estates and property were distributed to the Germans who flooded in to serve the Habsburgs, and of the cynical remark by Ferdinand III (1637–57) who said that, 'a Czech on the Charles Bridge of Prague would become as great a rarity as a stag with golden antlers.' In 1749 German was made the official language in Bohemia. When the Englishman Fyner Moryson visited Prague in 1617 he was already using the German name for the Vltava river: 'Moldau in the winter useth to be so frozen, as it beareth carts, and the ice thereof being cut in great peeces . . .' (The ice was used to cool wine in the royal cellars.)

From the bridge you can catch a glimpse of the Žofín Island where the nineteenth-century composer Antonín Dvořák, the illustrious son of a highly respected violin makers' family, played dance tunes in his youth. To the left of the island the Palladian style roof of the National Theatre glows in the rays of the setting sun. The theatre is a symbol of the National Revival which had begun in the 1780s. After more than 260 years of Germanization the Czechs decided to build their own cultural landmark where they could use their own language, perform their music and plays, and celebrate their own artists. The great Romantic poet Karel Hynek Mácha (1810–36) who died at the early age of twenty-six was performing in amateur theatres and writing

Czech poems full of fierce primitive love of beauty: 'I love flowers because they wither, animals because they die, Man because he knows that he is mortal and feels that he will perish forever, above all, I love – nay! worship God because he does not exist.' The Czech colours of red, blue and white became the compulsory chic. Women often wore national costumes and men like Tomáš Masaryk, who later became president of the first independent Czechoslovak Republic, smoked cigarettes rolled out of red, blue and white paper. The creation of a National Theatre, however, required money, and a fundraising campaign with the slogan, 'the Nation for Itself' began. People from all over the country contributed money, women brought their jewellery and poor weavers sent their finest linen to be sold for the purpose of raising the large amounts needed. The first building burnt down, but the second one, affectionately known as the 'little golden chapel' opened in 1883 with the aria of *Libuše*. 'My dear Czech people shall never die, but come through every horror with glory,' the public listened with tears to the words of the Smetana's opera. Almost all the leading Czech artists were involved in the decoration of this eloquent architectural expression of Czech nationalist aspirations.

Before entering the medieval streets of the Old Town it is worth examining the statue of Charles IV, another reminder of Prague's greatest ruler. Not only was he behind many of the city's architectural landmarks but he also introduced viniculture from France. After 600 years the vineyards he founded with vines imported from France are still here. We are a nation of beer drinkers who also happen to make a rather good wine thanks to Charles IV.

Following Charles Street I pass the complex of buildings of the Clementinum, the former Jesuit college, hidden behind its walls like a fortress. Its task was to re-Catholicise the Protestant population. Charles Patin quips in his *Travels . . .* in 1697, 'If the thirteen hundred apothecaries in London are a sufficient Evidence of its Populousness, the two thousand Jesuits of Prague may be cited to the like purpose . . .'

Finally I arrive at the Old Town Square and the Old Town Hall with its astronomical clock (the Orloj). It was here that twenty-seven Czech dignitaries were executed on 18 June 1621 for having led a revolt against the Habsburgs. Three were hanged and twenty-four decapitated. Their heads kept twitching and groaning after being separated from their torsos. Black scaffold, black masks and black cloaks of executioner's assistants the scene was 'an atrocious spectacle', the poet and essayist Dačický wrote. One of the men, Jessenius, the rector of the Prague University, had his tongue cut off before the execution. The Austrians dreaded his eloquence. (Milena Jesenská, the fearless woman journalist who defied the Nazis by helping the Jews and others during the German occupation, came from the same branch of the family.) To further spread the terror, the heads of twelve men were displayed on the towers of Charles Bridge. The Czech Protestant nobility had their estates and property confiscated, and was forced into exile. Today the pavement in the Old Town Square is marked with twenty-seven crosses.

One of the most striking features in the square is the partially hidden Church of Our Lady Before Týn which was first mentioned in the twelfth century. It belonged to the hospice of foreign merchants in the area known now as Ungelt. The Romanesque church was pulled down and during the reign of Charles IV foundations were laid for its Gothic replacement. This supremely elegant church is primarily associated with the followers of Jan Hus. One of its greatest benefactors was the Utraquist king, George of Poděbrady (1456–71), the last native ruler. The Hussites were divided into two groups: the Utraquists, who took over the established Church from its largely German, Catholic hierarchy, and the radical Táborites, who founded separate evangelical communities centred on Tabor, 50 miles south of Prague. The gable of the church was adorned with a statue of king George and a gold chalice symbolizing the Utraquist cause, but these were removed after the Protestants were defeated in 1620 and replaced with the statue of Virgin Mary, whose halo was made from the gold of the chalice.

Christian Andersen visited the church where he stood in front of the red-Slivenec marble sculpture of Tycho Brahe wearing a heavy armour, looking upwards, resting his right hand on an armillary sphere and gripping a sword with his left. Andersen pondered on the great Danish astronomer's fate. According to a legend Brahe died a grotesque death after suffering a burst bladder at a banquet.

Not only is the Týn Church the most impressive historical building on the right bank of the River Vltava but it has the most beautiful organ. In 1864 the funeral service of the composer of *Libuše*, Bedřich Smetana, was held here.

During the period between the two world wars President Tomáš Masaryk said in an interview with the writer Karel Čapek that, 'Lies and exaggerations are the worst propaganda of all. But to learn and to learn well you need love.' Another man who defended truth and whose monument is prominent in the square is that of Jan Hus whose motto, 'The Truth shall prevail' is embroidered today on the Czech presidential standard.

Between the Old Town Square and the river is the former Jewish quarter. The sixteenth century traveller Fynes Moryson gave a vivid description of the 'litle Citty', populated by 500 people. 'I had opportunity . . . not only to beholde the diuers Ceremonyes, of the Hussites, the Lutherans, the Papists, and the singular Jesuites, but also to haue free speech with the Jewes, and to enter their Synagoges at the tyme of divine service.' His account of various ceremonies, including a burial and a circumcision is full of detail, and through it the community comes to life in an instance. The labyrinthine ghetto was a mixture of small houses, extensions and arcades without identifying numbers and names. The property rights were equally complicated because the houses were divided, so that one family owned only a part of a given house, while another had a possession of the staircase, the cellar or some other structure.

At the turn of the twentieth century most of its picturesque houses and slums were demolished in a programme called 'sanitation'. Six synagogues including the fortress-like Old-New Synagogue, the town hall and the Old

Jewish Cemetery survived. Someone described the Cemetery as 'the sole garden of the Jewish Town, a garden of the dead, that still evokes the spirit of the ghetto defying the passage of intervening centuries.' Rabbi Loew, one of the greatest of Jewish thinkers and scholars is buried here. His tombstone reads: 'Rabbi Yehuda, son of Bezalel, the Lion, a great gaon in Israel, powerful with the "higher" and the "lower" / he entered everywhere with or without permission / passed through every garden of paradise untouched / he was wiser than any who learns and teaches the Law / nothing escaped his notice / he gathered together and united both great and small / he wrote endless works / and the yield of his labours was over fifteen books.' The last burial took place in 1787.

Stylish and beautiful apartment blocks embellished with Art Nouveau motifs replaced the medieval quarter. Franz Kafka, the man with a highly sensitized radar within his sickly body, wrote, 'In us it still lives – the dark corners, the secret alleys, shattered windows, squalid courtyards, noisy bars and sinister inns. We walk through the broad streets of the newly built town. But our steps and ours glances are uncertain. Inside we tremble . . .' He sensed the horror of the times ahead and died before the Second World War was unleashed. The Nazis murdered 84 per cent of Czech Jewry but they did not manage to obliterate the tradition of the Jewish Town. Apart from the Old-New Synagogue – still in use for worship – the remaining synagogues today serve exhibition purposes.

At the end of Parisian Street I can look at Letná hill, on the other side of the Čechův Bridge. It is empty now, but in 1962 it was the location of the largest monument to Stalin ever built, and in that year it was being demolished in front of my eyes. As a thirteen-year-old boy I stood here with my classmates and teachers watching the explosions. Nine years after Stalin's death, the Czechoslovak Communist hardliners were forced by Moscow's leaders to remove it. The massive structure consisting of nine figures (Stalin, four Russians and four Czechs), was being dismantled carefully, bit by bit, arms and heads first, the torsos later, over a period of several weeks. Later Stalin's head was driven through the streets of Prague like in some surreal artistic happening, like a flash forward of things to come. My parents saw the collapse of the Austro-Hungarian Empire and the defeat of the Third Reich, and I observed the disintegration of the Soviet Union.

As I wander through the Old Town markets, the Fruit Market and the Coal Market, I recall the American Marcia Davenport's sensual description of her olfactory experiences during her first visit in 1930. 'The Prague smell was a rich compound of coal smoke, roasting coffee, smoked pork and frying onions. A goose market day at the Coal Market, full of geese, both dressed and very much alive. A pandemonium of honks and hisses.' She ate a sausage grilled on a street-corner charcoal brazier with black bread, some Slovak *foie gras*, a slice of roasted piglet with dumplings and Czech pastries. Only an outsider like her would spot little details like *plzeň* beer always served in thin, tall, tapered glasses. Only a woman notices linen sheets and an 'oblong bag filled with the finest goose-down.'

Davenport returned to Prague and during the occupation through her Czech contacts she found out about the brutal treatment meted out to Prague students. She followed the fate of the deported Jews and after the war she monitored the Communist' shenanigans. Jan Masaryk met her in New York in 1941. Their friendship grew and after the war she came to Prague in an official capacity offering American aid to Czechoslovakia. She was a dangerous friend to cultivate in Stalinist Prague. The couple planned to escape to the West. She was safely out of the country when she was told of Jan Masaryk's murder.

Whenever I pass the Carolinum, the original building of the university which was founded by Charles IV in 1348, I cannot resist a visit to the Estates Theatre which is nearby. Here Pasqual Bondini introduced Mozart's *The Marriage of Figaro* to Prague audiences. It was a triumphal success and Bondini offered Mozart 100 guldens for a new opera to be written specifically for Prague. On 29 October 1787 the premiere of *Don Giovanni* became another of his triumphs. Although the musicians were nervous because their overture parts reached them just before the performance, Mozart, who conducted the opera, was received 'with the warmest approval,' as he later reported in a letter to his friend Jacquin.

My coffee stop at the Municipal House is a short break which brings memories from my childhood, during which many of my artistic activities centred on this elegant building. Although I am more of a beer drinker I do like the smell of coffee, the newspapers, the black-coated waiters and the whiff of pre-war elegance and Vienna. Franz Kafka who wrote his works in Prague German attended cafes, while Jaroslav Hašek, the author of *The Good Soldier Švejk* (which was written in Czech) went to pubs. Cafes of the 1920s were called by some the 'spiritual centres of the world' where in the clouds of smoke from unfiltered cigarettes the Czech avant-garde was born; where painters, architects, actors, journalists and others discussed a new building, an opera, a revolution or Hašek's latest article which uncovered mermaids and werewolves living just outside Prague as well as the establishment of his Party of Moderate Progress within the Bounds of Law.

The Municipal House is all about the exuberance of Bohemian arts. It is a showcase for the Bohemian *bohèmes* in the Art Nouveau style. Different artists worked in different parts of the House. The Mayor's Room was designed by Alfons Mucha who not only painted the allegory of Prague on the ceiling, featuring the most prominent Czech artists, but also designed the furniture and the curtains, embroidered with peacocks and studded with ruby-coloured beads. Mucha, famous the world over for his Sarah Bernhardt posters, died in 1939 after returning from an interrogation by the Gestapo.

As I leave through the main door, I often look up at the iron awning embellished with opal and stained glass. The Municipal House was built on the site of the Old Palace which was occupied by the Bohemian kings who travelled between this place and Hradčany, giving it the name of the 'Royal Route'. The building is also a symbol of the Czechs' national aspirations and the middle-classes wealth.

My personal tour of Prague ends at the Wenceslas Square, the heart of the New Town. It is not really a square, rather an avenue which is half a mile long. Originally a horse market, from the mid-nineteenth century the square became the stage for some key historic moments in the city's history. Some of the demonstrations which took place here were spontaneous, others were organized by terror. In 1918 a crowd gathered here to celebrate the country's newly regained independence and the collapse of the 300 year reign of the Habsburgs; its standards and symbols with the imperial double-headed eagle were torn and smashed. The new republic consisted of Bohemia, Moravia, Silesia and Slovakia. Its name was Czechoslovakia, it was a democracy and the seventh richest state in the world. Here in Wenceslas Square the people welcomed their democratic leaders, Tomáš Masaryk and Edvard Beneš when they arrived from exile. Masaryk, the first President of Czechoslovakia quoted Comenius who said that the governance of things would again return to the hands of his conquered nation. To Masaryk the new Europe was, 'like a laboratory built over the graveyard of the World War, and a laboratory calls for the cooperation of all. Democracy – modern democracy – is in its infancy,' he admitted later.

The twenty years of peace and democracy came to an abrupt end when the country was invaded by the Germans and re-named as the Protectorate of Bohemia and Moravia, while Slovakia, encouraged by the Nazis, declared its independence and became a fascist state. During the German occupation Prague lost her bravest fighters and the most patriotic intelligentsia. The Jews were sent to concentration camps via the transit camp of Terezín. The resistance members were tortured in the Petschek Palace, the Prague Gestapo headquarters not far from Wenceslas Square, or in Pankrác prison where in 1943 the Germans installed a guillotine. Men and women were beheaded at Pankrác or shot at the Kobylisy firing range. The rest of the population was encouraged to work hard for the armament industry and the German war effort on the Eastern Front.

When in 1942 two Czechoslovak soldiers sent from England, Jan Kubiš and Josef Gabčík, assassinated the acting Reichsprotektor Reinhard Heydrich, the inhabitants of Prague experienced an unprecedented wave of terror. The village of Lidice was razed to the ground, all the men were shot, and the women and children were sent to concentration camps. Later another village, Ležáky met a similar fate. After the assassination, Kubiš and Gabčík (together with five other Czech parachutists sent over from England) found a refuge in the Church of SS Cyril and Methodius on Resslova Street. In the early hours of 18 June, the Germans surrounded the church and a bloody battle ensued during which the Czechoslovak Soldiers were killed.

In retaliation a demonstration of loyalty to the Third Reich was forced on the terror-stricken inhabitants. It was here in Wenceslas Square in 1942 that the people were forced to sing their national anthem while holding their arms in a Nazi salute. In the last days of the war many young men joined the Prague Rising and on 9 May 1945 the city was liberated by the insurgents (with some help from the General Vlasov's white Russians) and the Soviet Army which came from Berlin. In the air scented by lilacs people in Wenceslas Square celebrated their freedom while the Russians danced *kazachok* to lively tunes played on accordions.

In the elections of 1946 the Communist Party of Czechoslovakia polled 38 per cent of the vote. The democrats were hoping to win at the next election scheduled for 1948. However, by 1947 Stalin's decisions were being forced on the non-Communist members of the government. It was becoming increasingly clear that the police, the security services and the army had been infiltrated by men trained in Moscow. In 1949 when the Communists took over control of the country in a bloodless coup, Klement Gottwald announced the creation of the Communist government at a mass rally in Wenceslas Square. Each year on the anniversary of the so-called 'Victorious February', Praguers had to participate in these compulsory celebrations while carrying portraits of Czechoslovak and Soviet Communist leaders, singing the 'International' and listening to endless speeches about the evil western imperialists who were conspiring to take over the world. The show trials of the early-1950s followed the Moscow model. It is estimated that in the course of this Stalinist terror over 100,000 people were incarcerated in prisons and labour camps built all over Czechoslovakia.

In the 1960s a gradual liberalization slowly made inroads. Political reforms by Alexander Dubček and others were being prepared to the fury of the Moscow hardliners. 'The Prague Spring' as the period came to be known, was brutally extinguished with a display of military power.

On the day of the Soviet invasion on 21 August 1968 the inhabitants of Prague realized that they were being 'ruled by gangsters' as Alexander Dubček simply put it. The Soviet tanks were transported by air and after landing at Ruzyně airport, they disembarked from the heavy Antonov planes and headed for the city centre. A number of them took up positions in Wenceslas Square. They fired at the National Museum, the Neo-Renaissance building behind the St Wenceslas statue, mistaking it for the Central Committee of the Communist Party (where the socialist reformers – the 'heretics' were based). The situation around the Prague radio station, just behind the National Museum looked even more dramatic when five tanks caught fire from their leaking fuel. Dubček and his colleagues were kidnapped and flown to Moscow. Eight days later they were returned beaten men. Their attempt at 'socialism with human face' was over, censorship was re-introduced and the invasion legalized.

Half a year later, on 16 January 1969, a twenty-year-old student from the Charles University, Jan Palach, set himself alight, a few yards from the statue of St Wenceslas, in protest against the Soviet occupation. He died three days later. One Prague inhabitant summed up the tragedy saying, 'What a country we live in, where the only light for the future is the burning body of a young man.'

On 17 November 1989 students marching from Narodní

Avenue to Wenceslas Square were attacked by armed riot police. The statue of Wenceslas was papered with posters and protest leaflets, and in front of it flowers and candles were placed in commemoration of Jan Palach. In the course of events that followed afterwards and which became known as the 'Velvet Revolution', Václav Havel addressed the crowds from the balcony of the Melantrich House further down the square. The former dissident, soon to become Czechoslovakia's new President, once wrote: 'One must not tolerate violence in silence in the hope that it will simply run its course.' During these public meetings the 1960s pop idol, Marta Kubišová, sang the national anthem and some of her moving songs that had been banned under Communist rule. Next to her on the Melantrich balcony stood Alexander Dubček, the man whom she publicly kissed in an open display of affection which resulted in her professional career being abruptly terminated by the authorities.

Nearly two decades later Prague is the capital of the Czech Republic which in 2004 became a new member state of the European Union.

Our tour started in the St Wenceslas Chapel in Prague Castle and it ends 'downtown' near the majestic monument to St Wenceslas (sculpted by Josef Václav Myslbek) situated at the top of a square named after the martyred Bohemian ruler. An inscription on the marble pedestal of this imposing equestrian statue reads: 'Saint Wenceslas, do not let us perish, nor our progeny' – a line from a prayer which became especially timely in the course of the turbulent twentieth century.

In 1918 Prague witnessed the end of the 300 year rule by the Habsburg dynasty and the collapse of the once mighty Austro-Hungarian Empire. For the next twenty years the new capital of Czechoslovakia enjoyed a brief but doomed period of democracy, peace and prosperity. During the nightmarish years of the German occupation from March 1939 until May 1945 when Prague was the longest Nazi-occupied city in Europe, the Nazis decimated a large number of her intelligentsia and murdered tens of thousands of her Jews, while Hitler's architect Albert Speer planned (but mercifully never realized) the transformation of Prague into a Berlin-style metropolis – a sort of Teutonic 'Gateway to the East'.

In the postwar years Prague was forced into the Communist orbit as the capital of one of the satellite states of the Soviet Empire, and then she was brutally invaded in August 1968 by the Soviets and their Eastern block allies crushing Alexander Dubček's 'socialism with a human face' experiment, followed by a political deep-freeze of the so-called 'normalization' process.

Finally in 1989, after fifty years of totalitarian rule, the Velvet Revolution of 1989 brought political freedom and relative prosperity with all the positive and negative aspects of a western-style democracy and free market economy, although many would argue that after a short honeymoon a new era of American domination, spirit-damaging consumerism, politics without ideals and aggressive brainwashing conducted through the media, was already on its way.

Prague could be sometimes compared to a great martial artist as she deflects and re-directs the blows aimed against her while preserving herself from damage and controlling aggression by not opposing it. She does not seek to humiliate her opponent or to establish her superiority but only to protect. Her great art counters violence and heals the people's dream-lives. Prague believes the universe is her home, and the sun, moon, the stars are her intimate friends. Not long ago, the Czech authorities issued a law protecting the beauty of stars by imposing a stiff fine on those who beam strong electric lights flooding the twinkling velvety sky. Prague defends the beauty of stars but Prague herself has to be protected by us.

CHARACTER OF
A CITY

[1] Following his visit to Prague in the beginning of the twentieth century, Auguste Rodin waxes lyrical about the hundred-spired city which reminds him of Dante's *Paradise*; from a letter to the organizers of the French sculptor's Prague exhibition in the spring of 1902.

Prague is a most majestic town and my mind frequently wandered to Rome – the city which resembles Prague more than any other. For completeness' sake, I would like to mention the splendour of a celebration, at which the aristocratic beauty of the Prague women, their magnificent gait and robes, so charming and elegant in the blooming spring gardens of the palace, reminded me of Dante's *Paradise*.

[2] The French historian Ernest Denis sees Prague in 1905 as a tragic city; from his preface to *Prague* by H. Hantich, Paris, 1906.

Florence is elegant and delicate as a design by Botticelli, and Venice is magnificent and voluptuous as a canvas by Titian. Paris is amicable, and strangers enjoy themselves there because everything breathes with smiling grace and the desire to charm. Vienna is joyous and frisky like one of Offenbach's operettas. Madame de Staël had said of Berlin that it was not a serious city, for the reason doubtless that it had grown too rapidly and that in its prosperity it was too brusque. Moscow with its picturesque and monotonous cupolas is hierarchical, and Bruges and Regensburg have the melancholic grandeur of ruins. PRAGUE IS TRAGIC. Every one of its stones recalls some heroic drama. Nowhere has life been fuller of torment, revolutions more numerous, passions more violent, combats more furious or more bitter. This is because nowhere have the interests at stake been more serious, and victory has seemed to the combatants to be more fraught with great consequences . . . Certain positions on the map assure to those who occupy them a measure of material superiority in the world. It is sufficient to cast one's eye on the map to realize that Prague is one of these posts which command history.

[3] During his visit to Prague in 1919 the British diplomat and spymaster Sir Robert Bruce Lockhart discovers important Czech-British historical links; from *Retreat from Glory*, London, 1934.

Here, every house had its history, a history written in the blood of religious wars. Here, too, were landmarks in the life-story of England. Here was the birthplace of Anne of Bohemia, the ill-fated consort of our own ill-fated Richard II. Here that dashing cavalry leader, Prince Rupert, had made his entry into the world. Here was unloosed the Thirty Years War between Catholic and Protestant, between Slav and German. Here the works of Wyclife, the inspirer of Hus, had been publicly burnt in front of the Archbishop's palace. Here, Žižka, the Czech Cromwell, had listened to the fiery counsels of Peter Payne, the English Taborite, who because of his origin was known as 'Magister Engliš' and whose part in the history of Czech Protestantism is commemorated in the Catholic song:

> The devil sent us Engliš;
> He creeps through Prague in Stealth,
> And whispers English doctrines,
> Unwholesome for our health.

Here, too, at the battle of the White Mountain in 1620 a Stuart Queen lost her throne. In that battle the Czech nation was deprived of its independence. Its lands were given to the Catholic invader. Its nobility disappeared. Its spirit had been enchained. But it had never been conquered. It still lived in the stone walls of the old city. Here was the Prague of Masaryk and of the countless Czech patriots, who during three hundred years of subjection had never ceased to lift their eyes to these silent sentinels of the past glory of their race. As a schoolboy I had been taught to sneer at Shakespeare's ignorance of geography in giving a seaboard to Bohemia. But Shakespeare had been more erudite than my professors. In the Middle Ages the kingdom of Bohemia, under the Přemyslides, had stretched from the Baltic to the Adriatic. Here in the soughing of the wind round the castle walls and in the lapping waters of the Vltava were the plaintive notes of the song which through the years of tribulation had kept alive the national spirit of the Czechs. The song of liberty is deathless. If there be no other merit in the Peace Treaties, they have, at least, restored to a sturdy, cultured race its birthright and its freedom.

The old and the new Prague represent that queer mixture of Slav mysticism and Teutonic materialism which form the basis of the Czech character. To me they were a stone and stucco symbol of the eternal struggle between the spirit and the flesh. In the secluded shelter of the old city I was happy and at peace. Across the river, calling more and more insistently, were the Nachtlokals of a materialist modern city drunk with the wine of its newly-won liberty. During my stay in Prague this struggle overshadowed my daily life, and in the process my character was to be weighed in the balance and found wanting.

[4] The veteran travel writer Patrick Leigh Fermor describes Prague in 1934 as 'one of the most beautiful and, at the same time, the strangest city in the world'; from *A Time of Gifts*, London, 1977.

Prague seemed – it still seems, after many rival cities – not only one of the most beautiful places in the world, but one of the strangest. Fear, piety, zeal, strife and pride, tempered in the end by the milder impulses of munificence and learning and *douceur de vivre*, had flung up an unusual array of grand and enigmatic monuments. The city, however, was scattered with darker, more reticent, less easily decipherable clues. There were moments when every detail seemed the tip of a phalanx of inexplicable phantoms. This recurring and slightly sinister feeling was fortified by the conviction that Prague, of all my halts including Vienna itself, was the place which the word Mitteleuropa, and all that it implies, fitted most aptly. History pressed heavily upon it. Built a hundred miles north of the Danube and three hundred east of the Rhine, it seemed, somehow, out of reach; far withdrawn into the conjectural hinterland of a world the Romans never

knew. (Is there a difference between regions separated by
this ancient test? I think there is.) Ever since their names
were first recorded, Prague and Bohemia had been the west-
ernmost point of interlock and conflict for the two greatest
masses of population in Europe: the dim and mutually ill-
disposed volumes of Slavs and Teutons; nations of which
I knew nothing. Haunted by these enormous shadows, the
very familiarity of much of the architecture made Prague
seem more remote. Yet the town was as indisputably a part
of the western world, and of the traditions of which the
West is most justly vain, as Cologne, or Urbino, or Toulouse
or Salamanca – or, indeed, Durham, which – on a giant
scale, *mutatis mutandis*, and with a hundred additions – it
fleetingly resembled.

[5] The Czech writer Heda Margolius Kovály finds a
unique relationship between Prague and the lives of
her people; from *I Do Not Want To Remember*, 1968.

Springtimes in Prague who could forget them? Forsythias on
the Letná plain; the chestnuts on Žofín; the gulls on Jirásek
bridge. There is no city like Prague. You have to wander to
the end of the earth to appreciate the magic that is not simply
the beauty of the buildings, of the towers and the bridges,
though it is that, too. They rise up from the ground in such
a natural harmony as if nature had created them, growing
out of the slopes and riverbanks like trees and flowers. But
what is unique about Prague is the relation between the city
and its people. Prague is not an eternal, uncaring backdrop,
which stands there through good and ill, ignoring happiness
and suffering alike. Prague lives in the lives of her people and
shares in them, and they repay her with love that we usually
reserve for humans.

PRAGUE

Early Beginnings

[6] The earliest tales of the origins of Prague are, like those of most other European cities, entirely mythical. So, let us begin with Princess Libuše and her famous prophesy; from *Smetana* by Brian Large, London, 1970.

One of the earliest references (to Libuše) is to be found in the eleventh-century Latin *Chronicon Bohemorum* written by the Canon of Prague, Cosmas (1045–1125), whose three-volume work dealing with the legends of Bohemia is the most important source concerning the origin and development of the Bohemian State.

Cosmas's writings are tales rather than history, but they undoubtedly formed a tradition, the earliest and most popular of which describes Krok, the pagan Bohemian prince who, in default of male descendants, ruled over the country with his three daughters, Kazi, Teta (or Lethka) and Libuše:

> Smaller in years but greater in wisdom . . . she was wonderful among women, chaste in body, righteous in her morals, second

to none as judge over the people, affable to all and even amiable, the pride and glory of the female sex, doing wise and manly deeds; but as nobody is perfect, this so praiseworthy woman was, alas, a soothsayer . . .

Cosmas describes Libuše's reign, her dispute with two nobles, her choice of Přemysl as consort and her founding of the City of Prague:

Standing on a rock on Vyšehrad in the presence of her husband and the elders of the people, and incited by the spirit of prophecy, Libuše uttered this prediction: 'I see a town, the glory of which will reach the stars. There is a spot in the forest, thirty strides from this village, which the River Vltava (the Moldau) encircles and which to the north the stream Brusnice secures by its deep valley; and to the south a rocky hill, which from its rocks takes the name of Petřín, towers above it . . . when you have reached the spot you will find a man in the midst of the forest who is working at a door-step for a house. And as even mighty lords bend before a low door, so from this event you shall call the town which you shall build – Praha. Thus they proceeded immediately to the ancient forest, and having found the sign which had been given them they built on this site Praha, the mistress of all Bohemia.

The date of the founding of Prague is uncertain, as is most information concerning this semi-mythical Princess. However, the legend in this form is the most ancient account that has come down to us and is the one upon which all subsequent ones are based over the next (thousand) years.

[7] A modern re-telling of the Princess Libuše legend; from *A Treasury of Tales from the Kingdom of Bohemia* by Eduard Petiška, Prague, 1994.

Once, long, long ago, a castle stood over the Vltava with wooden ramparts and a timbered palace within the ramparts. Later it was given the name Vyšehrad (in Czech – *the High Castle*). It stood on the right bank of the river on a tall cliff, the foot of which was lapped by restless waves.

The castle stood as firm as the will of the princes who ruled in it.

For it is said that here Prince Přemysl would sit on a stone princely throne and, with Princess Libuše, would receive reports from all over his country, here he gave judgments and advice.

Under his rule the country changed ever more quickly. Thick forests retreated before fields, and between the fields hard-working hands built settlements and forts and castles. Prince Přemysl advised his people well. The more forts and castles there were in the land the better the settlers could defend themselves against enemy invasion. In times of war they retreated behind the bulwarks and fortifications, built up supplies there and herded in their cattle. Behind the fortifications they preserved their lives and that of their families.

The tribe of the Czechs increased, and there was a need to find more and more places to settle. Princess Libuše, asked where the most suitable place would be for a new settlement, answered: 'Settle in a place where you will find the four elements in mutual harmony. Fertile, life-giving earth, pure water, healthy air and enough fuel for fire, where the trees afford both wood and shade. If harmony reigns amongst the elements, you will want for nothing.'

Many families then settled in the land according to Libuše's advice, and their fields yielded a rich harvest and their herds multiplied. A cheerful smoke rose to the heavens from the fireplaces of the new homes.

It is said that at that time the prince's servant Okrs approached him and asked for a place where he could build a castle for himself. Přemysl was fond of Okrs and he allowed him to build a castle west of the Vltava, on a site protected by the steepness of the banks and the water. It is said that the castle was named after its founder, Okrs. But in time the mouths of the people changed the name to Okoř.

But it was not a lucky star that shone on the building of Okoř castle. Of the family that settled there came Šárka, and from her came misery, hatred and treachery. In those

days many settlements and forts grew up. It was like a
starry night when a multitude of stars shine, but the moon,
that surpasses all the stars in brightness and magnitude,
that rules over them, has not yet come up.

Once when Prince Přemysl visited Libušín castle with
Princess Libuše, they mounted together with their company
to the highest point of the castle. It was evening, and in the
glow of the setting sun the landscape spread out on all sides,
showing traces of the work of human hands. Fields alter-
nated with settlements and pastures, the forest had retreated
to the horizon and there held guard in close formation. The
dazzling sun was descending into the forest and the shadow
of the castle fell to the east. Princess Libuše turned to the
hazy blue shadows of advancing night and suddenly everything on the earth and in the atmosphere was seized by a
great silence. No one of the company spoke, the wind held
its breath and the birds, that had been warbling till that
moment, fell silent in the tree tops. The princess stretched
out her hand to the east, and as if she were touching something far away in the clouds and evening mists, she moved
her fingers gently and spoke:

'I see a great castle and its glory reaches to the stars. The
place lies hidden in deep woods, from the north it is protected by the valley of the Brusnice stream, from the south
by a wide rocky hill. The river Vltava pushes its way beneath
its slopes. Go there and in the midst of a wood you will see
a man hewing out threshold. There build a castle and name
it, according to the hewn threshold, Praha (in Czech *práh –
threshold*). And as even great men bow their heads on a
threshold, so will they bow them before this castle.'

Prince Přemysl and his company looked in that direction,
but all they saw was the advancing night. The future was
hidden in it like a precious stone in a hill. For a further
moment the Princess's white hand pointed into the distance,
then the prophetic spirit left her and the sparkle of her eyes
was extinguished. And, as happens with prophets and poets,
when Libuše's enthusiasm faded, it was awakened in those
who listened to her, and they started at once to prepare for
their journey.

At the break of a new day messengers set off towards the east, to find the place the Princess had spoken of. They came to the valley of the stream and to the rocky hill and entered the wood, from which regular blows could be heard. They found a man hewing out the threshold of a house.

They did not hesitate and went to work. They felled trees, built log-huts, raised earthworks. Thus on the left bank of the Vltava Prague castle grew up, wooden like Vyšehrad, but more spacious and more splendid. The name Praha spread from mouth to mouth throughout the length of the land, and foreign merchants, carried it to distant countries.

[8] A light-hearted look at an early feminist legend about Prague's own amazons; from *When Women Ruled in Prague*, by Karen von Kunes, Prague, 1999.

After the death of the legendary prophetess Libuše, ruler of the Czechs, women were exposed to men's ridicule and decided to fight back. Led by Libuše's comrade Vlasta, the story goes, they built a fortress on Děvín, a hill across the river from Vyšehrad. Its name bears the imprint of these warrior women: It's derived from *děva*, 'girl' in old Czech (*dívka* in the modern tongue).

The fight that followed was bloody, due not so much to the women's strength as to their cunning. The most seductive girls lured men from Vyšehrad to Děvín, where a whole army of women hid ready to attack. Many men died under the storm of sharp arrows loosed by the women.

This tale has survived in the names of streets under the hill, such as *Děvínská*, 'Girls' Street,' *U dívčích hradů*, 'At the Girls' Fortresses,' and *Šárčina*, 'Šárka's Street.' The Šárka commemorated in this street name was a shrewd girl who helped bring about the death of Ctirad, a strong young warrior. He found her tied to a tree, and she pleaded for release, saying the other women had bound her. When he freed her and blew the horn she carried, Ctirad fell into the trap as women swarmed out and captured him. His cruel death by torture on the wheel enraged the men, who – led by the Prince Vladimír – then conquered the women and destroyed their fortress Děvín. (In the Middle Ages, a castle was built on the same hill. Later it was used for artillery practice, and no trace of it remains.)

While this story is not particularly encouraging to feminists, it has become a part of Czech mythology, celebrated in literature, song and folklore.

First Impressions

[9] The first written record of a visit to Prague by a foreign observer comes from c. 965; from a manuscript (in Arabic) by Ibrahim-ibn-Jakub, a Jewish merchant and slave-trader from Moorish Spain, who travelled in 'the lands of the Western Slavs' in the tenth century.

The city of Prague is built of stone and lime and made richer by commerce than all others. From the city of Cracow the Russians and the Slavs arrive here with goods and from the lands of the Turks the Moslems and the Jews and the Turks also arrive to Prague with their merchandise and the coin of commerce taking away with them slaves, tin and various furs.

Their land is the best among the people of the north and the best-stocked in food. A wheat is sold here for one denarius in a quantity that it will last man for a month; a barley is sold for one denarius in a volume for a fodder for a horse for forty nights, and for one denarius they sell you ten hens.

In the city of Prague they manufacture saddles, bridles and made in a hurry, shields, which they use in their countries. In

the country of Bojm light handkerchiefs are made from a thin
net fabric and they are not useful for anything. The price for
one denarius is ten handkerchiefs. They sell and purchase
using the handkerchiefs. They own pots full of them. With
them they buy wheat, flour, horses, gold, silver and other
objects. One peculiarity is that Bohemian people are of dark
complexion with black hair and no blondes or redhead are
there.

Their women, when married, do not commit adultery.
But a girl, when she falls in love with some man or other,
will go to him and quench her lust. If a husband marries a
girl and finds her to be a virgin, he says to her, 'If there were
something good in you, men would have desired you, and
you would certainly have found someone to take your vir-
ginity.' Then he sends her back, and frees himself from her.

[10] A late sixteenth-century description of Prague;
from *Civitates Orbis Terrarum*, Georg Braun and
Franz Hogenberg, 1602.

The province of Bohemia is bounded on the north by
Germany, on the east by Hungary, by Bavaria on the south
and on the west by the Nordgaue. The Hercynian Forest [*the
Harz*] surrounds the country like a natural barrier. Through
the midst of it flows the Elbe, but the Moldau [*Vltava*] is
larger. On the latter is situated Prague, the noble capital of
the whole kingdom, which was called Bubienum and
Marobudum by Aventino, but Casturgis by Ptolemy. The
town was fortified by walls and ramparts by Przemysl II,
Duke of Bohemia and his consort Libussa. In Bohemian it is
called Praha. Now it is actually the seat of a king and the see
of a bishop, no less than Florence in Etruria. The city consists of three separate parts: Little Prague, Old Prague and
New Prague. Little Prague is on the left bank of the Moldau
and it adjoins the mountain on which stand the royal castle
and the cathedral of St Vitus. Old Prague is on level ground,
with magnificent and ornate buildings. Among them the
court of justice, the market place, the town hall and the
Caroline college are particularly esteemed. The old town is

connected with Little Prague by a stone bridge of twenty-four arches over the Moldau. But the new town is divided from Old Prague by a deep moat and fortified by walls. It is extensive and reaches as far as the hills, which are called St Charles, St Catherine and Wissegrad. On the latter there is a castle with a college, and its provost is the chancellor and prince of the whole kingdom. So writes Aeneas Sylvius. Charles, the fourth king of Bohemia, founded a university in Prague, with a valuable library and magnificent colleges. It was very seriously damaged by the senseless rage of the Hussites, but was restored by the Emperors Ferdinand and Maximilian II, and is now famous because of the many arts and sciences in which the students are instructed.

[11] The traveller Fynes Moryson visits Prague in the late sixteenth century; from *An Itinerary*, 1617, London, 1907–1908.

(Moryson was an Englishman who, after graduating from Cambridge, decided to 'gaine experience by travelling into forraigne parts'.)

On the West side of Molda [*Vltava*] is the Emperours Castle, seated on a most high Mountaine, in the fall wherof is the suburbe called Kleinseit, or little side. From this Suburbe to goe into the City, a long stone bridge is to be passed over Molda, which runnes from the South to the North, and divides the suburbe from the City, to which as you goe, on the left side is a little City of the Jewes, compassed with wals, and before your eies towards the East, is the City called new Prage, both which Cities are compassed about with a third, called old Prage. So as Prage consists of three Cities, all compassed with wals, yet is nothing lesse then strong, and except the stinch of the streets drive back the Turkes, or they meet them in open field, there is small hope in the fortifications thereof. The streets are filthy, there be divers large market places, the building of some houses is of free stone, but the most part are of timber and clay, and are built with little beauty or Art, the walles being

all of whole trees as they come out of the wood, the which
with the barke are laid so rudely, as they may on both sides
be seen.

[12] Hester Lynch Piozzi arrives 'safe' in Prague in 1789;
from *Observations and Reflections*, London, 1789.

*(Harriet Lynch Thrale née Salusbury [1741–1821] was
born near Pwllheli, Gwynedd. In 1763 she married Henry
Thrale, a prosperous brewer. Dr Samuel Johnson conceived
an extraordinary affection for her, and lived in her house at
Streatham Place for over sixteen years. After her husband
died, Hester became attached to the Italian musician
Gabriel Piozzi, whom she married in 1784 – with Dr
Johnson feeling somewhat slighted as a consequence.)*

The inns between Vienna and this place are very bad; but we
arrived here safe the 24th of November, when I looked for
little comfort but much diversion; things turned out however
exactly the reverse, and *aux bains de Prague* in Bohemia we
found beds more elegant, dinners neater dressed, apartments
cleaner and with less foreign aspect, than most any where
else. Such is not mean time the general appearance of the
town out of doors, which is savage enough; and the celebrated bridge singularly ugly I think, crowded with vast
groupes of ill-made statues, and heavy to excess, though not
incomodious to drive over, and of a surprising extent. These
German rivers are Magnificent, and our Mulda [*Vltava*] here
(which is but a branch of the Elbe neither) is respectable for
its volume of water, useful for the fish contained in it, and
lovely in the windings of its course.

[13] In a short story inspired by his visit in 1902,
the French poet Guillaume Apollinaire sets out to
explore Prague in the company of Isaac Laquedem,
who claims to be the legendary 'Wandering Jew'; from
Le Paesant de Prague translated by Pascal Thivillon,
Paris, 1967.

We visited the royal castle of Hradschin with its majestic and
desolate rooms, then the cathedral, which houses the royal
tombs and the silver shrine of Saint Nepomuk. In the vault,
where the kings of Bohemia were crowned, and where Saint
King Wenceslas became a martyr, Laquedem pointed out that
the walls were made of gems. He showed me an amethyst:
'Look at the centre, the veining is like a face with flamboyant
and mad eyes. One could say it is the mask of Napoleon.'

'It's my face,' I cried, staring at it with my dark and jealous
eyes! And it was true. Here it was, my painful portrait, close
to the bronze door where the ring hangs that Saint Wenceslas
was holding when he was murdered. We had to leave. I was
pale and distressed to have seen myself mad [. . .]

Night was falling and lights were appearing in the city.
We crossed the Moldau [*Vltava*] again by a more modern
bridge: 'It is dinner time,' Laquedem said, 'walking stimu-
lates the appetite and I am a big eater.'

We entered an inn where music was playing. There was
a violinist; a man who held a drum, bass drums and a tri-
angle; a third man who played a kind of harmonium with
two small keyboards in juxtaposition and placed on top of
bellows. These three musicians made a hellish racket and
accompanied very well the *goulasch* with paprika, the fried
potatoes with cumin seeds, the bread with poppy seeds and
the bitter Pilsen lager that was served to us.

We left the inn and crossed the big rectangular square
named Wenzelplatz, Viehmarkt, Rossmarkt or Václavské
Náměstí. It was ten o'clock. Women were lurking in the
glow of the street lights, murmuring Czech words of invita-
tion. Laquedem took me to the Jewish city, saying: 'You will
see: for the night, each house is transformed into a brothel.'

[14] A young diplomat takes up his post at the British
Legation in Prague in 1919; from *Retreat from Glory*
by R. H. Bruce Lockhart, London, 1934.

My first impressions of Prague were mixed. Looking back
to-day after a residence there of nearly seven years, I find
the same curious difficulty in forming a definite opinion.

There are moments when its beauty haunts me to the exclusion of all other beautiful cities. There are other occasions, when some baleful curse seems to emanate from its cobbled alleys and when its rococo gargoyles gibber and mock. The fault is perhaps my own. In Prague lies the wreckage of the last years of my youth.

I arrived, if not as a conqueror, at least in some of the reflected glory of the victorious Allies. I came, too, alone, and my wife did not join me until seven months later. In that winter of 1919–20 conditions of life in Central Europe were still uncomfortable and unsettled. The railway system had not yet begun to function, and I travelled from Paris in a special military train. The journey took the best part of three days, and our route lay through Switzerland and Austria.

I arrived at Prague late in the evening and was met on the platform by John Latter, a nephew of General Sir Nevil Macready and then Third Secretary at our Legation. Here all was bustle and efficiency. The station, re-christened by the Czechs in gratitude for their newly-won independence the Wilson station [*formerly the Franz Josef I station*], was crowded with Czech porters, Czech legionaries, Czech Jans, Antons, and Karels, which are the Czech equivalents for our Tom, Dick and Harry. The station was now their station. The trains were their trains. The fruits of independence and of possession had not yet lost their savour.

I collected my luggage and drove off with Latter to my hotel. At break-neck speed we passed through the Hoover Gardens, past the Historical Museum and the huge statue of St Wenceslas, down the wide Wenceslas Place into the Poříč. The street lamps revealed buildings, mostly shops and offices. The pavements were thronged with men and women. They looked happy, well-fed, but undistinguished. My first impression was of a Belgian provincial town. I was in the business quarter. It did not attract me then. I do not like it to-day.

In a few minutes we drew up before a cold, barrack-looking building with the sign 'Hotel Imperial' surmounting its circular swinging door. My heart sank. In apologetic tones Latter explained that Prague was filled to overflowing. There were as yet no new hotels. Those that existed offered merely a choice of evils. Tomorrow, we should see about a house or a flat. The Government would help. There was a big reception that night at the Municipal House. If I liked to change, he would wait for me and introduce me to the *Corps Diplomatique* and to the various Czech ministers. I pleaded tiredness, unpacked my belongings, and retired to bed. The blinds did not work. The light of the street lamps and the noise of the street-cars below my window kept me awake for hours. I spent a restless and unhappy night.

The next morning the sky was blue, and, as I waited for the car which was to take me to the Legation, the keen, winter air stirred me to a new energy. That drive was a memorable one. In a few seconds I had passed from the modern materialism of the business quarter into a new world. Its gate was the old Powder Tower. Its streets – narrow cobbled alleys, flanked with the baroque palaces of the aristocrats were full of mystery. They twined and twisted, ending sometimes in ridiculous culs-de-sac with a postern and a grinning gargoyle barring further progress. On our way we passed through the Old Town Square with its great statue of Jan Hus and its old Town Hall with its clock and performing apostles, who make their round as every hour strikes, past the University, where Hus was rector, past the colossal statue of Charles IV, greatest of all Czech kings and son of that John of Luxembourg who fell at Crécy and from whose shield the Prince of Wales gets his three feathers and his motto, 'Ich Dien', down on to the glorious Charles Bridge with its stone buttresses and its statues of the saints. There, glittering in the winter sun, was the Prague which I had imagined in my dreams. Below my feet was the Vltava, its slow waters studded with picturesque islands, and behind the river rising up from the water's edge to the summit of high hills, Old Prague with its castle, its palaces, its churches, its ridiculous staircase streets, and its hanging gardens. As I crossed the bridge, I felt as if I were entering fairyland. Gone was all the twentieth century shoddiness. Here was the home of romance – that romance which has inspired The Witch of Prague, The Winter Queen, Golem, and a score of other histories and novels of the Middle Ages. Here, too, hidden somewhere between the base, formed by the river and the Wallenstein Palace, and the apex of St. Vitus's Cathedral, with its quaint Alchemists' Alley behind it, lay the Thun Palace, now the home of the British Legation and my new headquarters. Here in this fairy-city, more beautiful than any city I have ever seen, was the soul of Prague.

[15] Patrick Leigh Fermor walks into Prague in 1934; from *A Time of Gifts*, London, 1977.

Stripped of the customary approach on foot, Prague remains distinct from all the other towns on this journey. Memory encircles it with a wreath, a smoke-ring and the paper lattice of a valentine. I might have been shot out of a gun through all three of them and landed on one of its ancient squares fluttering with the scissor-work and the vapour and the foliage that would have followed me in the slipstream. The trajectory had carried Hans and me back in the middle of winter. All the detail – the uprush of the crockets, the procession of statues along the coping of bridges and the levitated palaces – were outlined with snow; and, the higher the buildings climbed, the more densely the woods enfolded the ancient town. Dark with nests, skeleton trees lifted the citadel and the cathedral above the tops of an invading forest and filled the sky with cawing and croaking . . . The city teems with wonders.

Seen from a fountain-square of the Hradčany, the green copper domes, where each snow-laden segment is pierced with a scrolled lunette, might belong to great Rome itself. The pinnacles on all the cupolas are tipped with monstrances shooting rays like golden fireworks; and when these and the gold balls on the tips of the other finials are touched by a rare sunbeam, the air glitters for a moment with a host of flying baubles.

A first glance, then, reveals a baroque city loaded with the spoils of the Austrian Caesars. It celebrates the Habsburg marriage-claims to the crown of Bohemia and reaffirms the questionable super-session of the old elective rights of the Bohemians; and alongside the Emperor's temporal ascendancy, this architecture symbolizes the triumph of the Pope's Imperial champion over the Hussites and the Protestants. Some of the churches bear witness to the energy of the Jesuits. They are stone emblems of their fierce zeal in the religious conflict.

[16] In August 1936, Albert Camus spent four 'deadly' days full of 'anguish' alone in a cheap hotel room in Prague; from his *Diaries*, translated by Pascal Thivillon, Paris.

I arrived in Prague at six in the evening. Immediately, I left my bags at the left-luggage office. I had two hours remaining to look for a hotel. And I was overwhelmed by a strange feeling of freedom as my two suitcases were no longer weighing me down. I left the station, walked by some gardens and suddenly found myself thrown into Wenceslas avenue, bubbling with people at this time of the day. Around me, a million beings who have lived until now without me being aware of their existence. They were living. I was thousands of kilometres away from my own country. I didn't understand their language. They walked quickly. Passing me, they left me behind. I was out of my depth.

I was short of money. Enough to live on for six days. But, by then, someone was supposed to join me. Nevertheless, I was anxious about this matter. So I began to search for a modest hotel. I was in the new town and all those that I saw sparkled with lights, laughter and women. I went more quickly. Something in my frantic pace already resembled an escape. Around eight, tired, I arrived in the old town. There, a modest-looking hotel, with a small entrance, attracted me. I enter. I fill in my form. I take my key. I have room No 34, on the third floor. I open the door and find myself in a luxurious room. I look for an indication of price: it is twice as much as I thought. The question of money becomes a thorny issue. I can only manage to live poorly in this big town.

[. . .] I explored the town methodically. I lost myself in the sumptuous baroque churches, trying to rediscover there a homeland, but leaving more empty and more desperate by this delusive *tête-à-tête* with myself. I wandered along the Vltava cut by over-flowing dams. I spent a disproportionate amount of time in the vast district of Hradschin, now deserted and silent. In the shadow of its cathedral and palaces, as the sun was setting, my solitary footsteps made the streets resonate. Noticing this, I again began to panic. I dined early and went to bed at half-past eight. The sun brought me out of myself. Churches, palaces and museums; I tried to relieve my anxiety in all the works of art. The usual trick: I wanted to turn my rebellion into melancholy. But in vain. As soon as I left, I was a stranger. One time, however, in a baroque cloister, at the far end of the city, the peacefulness of the hour, the slow chimes of the bells, the clusters of pigeons flying from the old tower, and something about the smell of grass and emptiness gave birth to a silence inside me that filled with tears, that brought me close to freedom. Back at night, I immediately wrote down the words that follow, that I faithfully transcribed, because in their pomposity I found a complexity similar to the one I was feeling at the time: And what other benefit can one expect from travel? Here I am stripped of my finery. A town where I cannot read the signs, strange characters where nothing familiar sticks, without friends to talk to, and ultimately without entertainment.

Now I can say what remains with me of Prague: it's the smell of pickled cucumbers that are sold at every street corner as a snack, the sour and pungent odour that awoke and accentuated my anxiety as soon as I left the door of my hotel. This and also perhaps an accordion melody. Under my windows, a blind, one-armed man sat on his instrument, holding it on one side with his bum cheek and playing with his good hand. It was always the same childish and tender melody that awoke me in the morning and brought me abruptly into the bleak reality in which I struggled.

In Prague, I suffocated between the walls.

THE CASTLE AND HRADČANY

The Legend of
St Wenceslas

---

[17] The life and martyrdom of St Wenceslas *c.935*; from old Slav legends.

(Born c.903, Duke Wenceslas [in Czech Václav] received a Christian education and after the death of his father [c.924] encouraged Christianity in Bohemia. In c.935 he was murdered by his brother Boleslav. Because so little is known, legends abound. Wenceslas became the patron saint of the Czech nation and an object of political mythology.)

There was a certain prince in Bohemia named Vratislav, and his wife was Drahomíra. Being delivered of her firstborn son, they Christened him and gave him the name Václav. And the infant grew, being protected by the clemency of God. He was greatly learned in Slavonic and Latin letters. When his father died, the Czechs made this Václav, his son, their prince. Boleslav, his brother, grew with him, for both were still small. But their mother, Drahomíra, strengthened the country and administered the wants of the people, until Václav grew up; and when he had grown, he began to rule the people himself.

By the goodness of God Václav was not only well instructed by many books, but the faith in him was perfect. When the Devil entered their hearts, the men of Bohemia disdainfully rose against their lord Václav. And they courted Boleslav, saying: 'Brother Václav seeks to kill thee.' Whenever there was a 'consecration of a church' in the castles, Václav rode out to them all. He came thus to the castle of Boleslav on Sunday and it was the feast of Cosmas and Damián; having heard Mass, he prepared to journey home to Prague. Boleslav, however, detained him, thinking evilly, saying: 'Why goest thou, when I have good drink!' When night had come these evil enemies met at the court of a certain murderer, Hněvys, and having summoned Boleslav, repeated that unfriendly council about his brother . . . then they said: 'When he goes to matins, then shall we watch for him.' When it was day the bells tolled for matins. Then Václav, hearing the bells, said: 'Praise to Thee, Lord, Who has granted me to live to this morn!' And rising, he went to matins. Immediately Boleslav shadowed him at the gates. Václav then looked upon him and said: 'Brother, thou wert our good servant yesterday.' Boleslav, as if the Devil whispered in his ear, drew his sword, and answered him, saying: 'Now I wish to be still a better to thee!' Having thus said, he struck him over the head with his sword. Václav turning to him, said: 'What is thy intent, brother?' And grasping him, threw him to the ground. And then a certain Tuža took courage and struck Václav on the hand. He, being wounded on the hand, released his brother, and fled to the church. Two murderers, however, called Tira and Česta, killed him at the door of the church.

St Vitus' Cathedral

[18] Hester Lynch Piozzi visits St Vitus' Cathedral in 1789; from *Observations and Reflections*, London, 1789.

The cathedral I am sure is an *old* thing, and charged with heavy and ill-chosen ornaments worthy of the age in which it was fabricated! – One would be loth to see any alteration take place, or any picture drive old Frank's Three Kings, divided into three compartments, from its station over the high altar. St John Neppomucene has an altar here all of solid silver, very bright and clean; his having been flung into river Mulda [*Vltava*] in the persecuting days, holding fast his crucifix and his religion, gives him a rational title to veneration among the martyrs, and he is considered as the tetular saint here, where his statuette meets one at the entrance to every town.

This truly Gothic edifice was very near being destroyed by the King of Prussia, who bombarded the city thirty-five years ago, I saw the mark by one ball just at the cathedral door; and heard with horror of the dreadful siege, when an egg was sold for a florin, and other eatables in proportion; the whole town has, in consequence of that long blocklade, a ragged and half-ruined melancholy aspect; and the roads round it, then broken up, have scarcely been mended since.

[19] In 1858 the novelist George Eliot finds the cathedral a 'melancholy object'; from *The Journals of George Eliot*, edited by Margaret Harris and Judith Johnson, 1998.

After dinner we took a carriage and went across the wonderful bridge of St Jean Nepomuk with its avenue of statues, towards the Radschin [*sic*] – an ugly straight-lined building but grand in effect from its magnificent site, on the summit of an eminence crowded with old massive buildings. The view from this eminence is one of the most impressive in the world – perhaps as much from one's associations with Prague as from its visible grandeur and antiquity. The Cathedral close to the Radschin is a melancholy object on the outside – left with unfinished sides like scars.

The interior is rich, but sadly confused in its ornamentation, like so many of the grand old churches – hideous altars of bastard style disgracing exquisite Gothic columns.

. . . Close in front of us sloping downwards was a pleasant orchard; then came the river with its long, long bridge and grand gateway; then the sober-coloured city with its surrounding plain and distant hills.

[20] In 1934, a young traveller from England explores St Vitus'; from *A Time of Gifts* by Patrick Leigh Fermor, London, 1977.

As I followed Hans's zigzag and switchback course all over the steep city, it occurred to me that hangovers are not always harmful. If they fall short of the double-vision which turns Salisbury Cathedral into Cologne they invest scenery with a lustre which is unknown to total abstainers. Once we were under the lancets of St Vitus's Cathedral, a second conviction began to form. Prague was the recapitulation and the summing-up of all I had gazed at since stepping ashore in Holland, and more; for that slender nave and the airy clerestory owed spiritual allegiance far beyond the Teutonic heartland, and the Slav world. They might have sprung up in France under the early Valois or in Plantagenet England.

The last of the congregation were emerging to a fickle momentary sunlight. Indoors the aftermath of incense, as one might say with a lisp, still floated among the clustered piers. Ensconced in their distant stalls, an antiphonal rear-guard of canons was intoning Nones.

Under the diapered soffits and sanctuary lamps of a chantry, a casket like a brocaded ark of the covenant enclosed the remains of a saint. Floating wicks and rows of candles lit up his effigy overhead: they revealed a mild medieval sovereign holding a spear in his hand and leaning on his shield. It was Good King Wenceslas, no less. The confrontation was like a meeting with Jack the Giant Killer or Old King Cole . . . English carol-singers, Hans told me as we knelt in a convenient pew, had promoted him in rank. The sainted Czech prince – ancestor of a long line of Bohemian kings, however – was murdered in 934. And there he lay, hallowed by his countrymen for the last thousand years.

Outside, except for the baroque top to the presiding belfry, the cathedral itself might have been an elaborate gothic reliquary. From the massed upward thrust of its buttresses to the stickleback ridge of its high-pitched roof it was spiked with a forest of perpendiculars. Up the corner of the transepts, stairs in fretted polygonal cylinders spiralled and counter-spiralled, and flying buttresses enmeshed the whole fabric in a radiating web of slants. Borne up in its flight by a row of cusped and trefoiled half-arches, each of them carried a steep procession of pinnacles and every moulding was a ledge for snow, as though the masonry were perpetually unloosing volleys of snow-feathered shafts among the rooks and the bruise-coloured and quicksilver clouds.

A spell hangs in the air of this citadel – the Hradčany, as it is called in Czech; Hradschin in German – and I was under its thrall long before I could pronounce its name.

Even now, looking at photographs of the beautiful lost city, the same spell begins to work.

[21] St Vitus' Cathedral – a 'guided tour' by a former British Ambassador to Prague; from *The Serpent and The Nightingale* by Sir Cecil Parrot, London, 1977.

(Sir Cecil was British Ambassador in Prague from 1960 to 1966.)

Next door to the Castle the great Cathedral of St Vitus towered above us (the British Embassy in Prague). It was one of my favourite haunts not only when I walked alone but when I took guests with me.

The cathedral was better than a Czech history book. It had taken longer to complete than any other church in the world. Founded in the tenth century by 'Good King Wenceslas' (Svatý Václav to the Czechs; no king, but a prince, and no old man with white hair, but a boy), it later became the shrine for his tomb, and was finally completed in the year 1929, the presumed millenary of his death. One of the last sections of the cathedral to be completed were the enormous bronze doors which carried what amounted to a strip cartoon of the saint's life. Four relief panels in bronze tell his story. In the first he is shown picking grapes in a vineyard, because he was so pious that he prepared the sacramental wine with his own hands. In the next he can be seen uniting and consolidating the Czech tribes into one Czech state, and, then, in the panel below, helping the poor ('Yonder peasant, who is he?'). This brief biography ends with his murder on his birthday by his brother Boleslav, who usurped the throne.

In the centre of the cathedral lie, as though by proprietorial right, the stone effigies of three important members of the Habsburg dynasty. In the middle, Ferdinand I, the ardent Spanish-born Catholic, who was the first Habsburg to rule Bohemia; on his left his wife, the Polish Anna of Jagellon, the daughter of the previous king; and on his right, their son, Maximilian II, on whom the Czech people vainly pinned their hopes because he had favoured Protestantism before his accession.

In the semicircular aisle alongside or behind the choir, more and more of Bohemia's history unfolds. The effigies of the medieval Přemysl rulers lie in the side altars. On the right stands the monumental and elaborate silver tomb of St John of Nepomuk, designed by Fischer von Erlach. Its material strikingly symbolizes Bohemia's wealth and power, which derived from her rich silver mines. As if to confirm this, two figures with miners' lamps peer out eerily from underneath the curious 'baroque' Gothic Royal Oratory of King Vladislav, Ferdinand's father-in-law.

How did St John of Nepomuk come to merit so important a tomb? He was the saint of the Jesuits and the Counter-Reformation, whose cult was imposed on the Czechs in a vain effort to break their allegiance to the reformer, Jan Hus, or even to the non-denominational national saint, St Wenceslas. In this fantastic tomb, which is a marvel of the silversmith's art, two aspects of the legend of the saint are combined. We see him as the queen's confessor, and, later, thrown into the Vltava from the Charles Bridge at the king's orders: another defenestration, or perhaps 'depontition'!

The Nepomuk legend became a live political issue in the nineteenth and twentieth centuries, when it was used by the anti-clericals to ridicule the traditional beliefs of the then influential Catholic Party. Jan of Pomuk was a real person. He was the administrator of the church in the reign of King Wenceslas IV, the son of the Emperor Charles. The king, after quarrelling with his bishop, was afraid to punish him and vented his wrath on the administrator instead, whom he ordered to be hanged, drawn and quartered and then thrown into the river. The Jan of the legend was a mystical martyr, a Jan of Nepomuk, who had refused to reveal what the Queen had confessed to him, when the king ordered him to do so. Hence his martyrdom. St John was elevated into the symbol of the inviolability of the confession and now stands for eternity with his finger on his lip, not only in Prague but all over Central Europe. What is the meaning of the stars round his crown? When his body, or rather bits of it, was being thrown over the bridge, awesome miracles took place, which the stars are supposed to symbolize. The legendary place of his 'depontition' is marked by a seventeenth-century plaque on the Charles Bridge.

More 'strip cartoons', this time panels of carved wood, show the acts of vandalism committed by the unpopular Calvinist chaplain of Frederic, the 'Winter King'. We see him hacking away at everything beautiful – another effective piece of Jesuit propaganda, but true. The companion panel shows the flight of Frederic and Elisabeth Stuart, his English Queen, after their defeat at the Battle of the White Mountain in 1620. There they go, lock, stock and barrel – almost forgetting, in their haste, their Prague-born son, the Cavalier Prince Rupert – and good riddance to them, as the picture clearly conveys.

A distinguishing feature of the cathedral is the St Wenceslas chapel, built by the Luxemburg king and emperor, Charles IV, who introduced the cult of St Wenceslas into Bohemia, having spent his childhood in the French court under the influence of the cult of Saint Louis. The chapel lies directly above the original tomb of the Czech saint and martyr. On its walls are mural paintings depicting further scenes from his life. Particularly interesting is the painting showing him chopping down the gallows and razing the prisons. It was said of him that he could not bear to remain in the council chamber when death sentences were passed, and always hurried out. The beautiful polychrome statue of St Wenceslas from the workshop of Peter Parler, the second builder of the cathedral, is one of the most precious adornments of the cathedral. Although its colours have faded, it shows St Wenceslas as he was seen at the time – possibly Charles's own conception of him – young, gentle and dreamy and, although girt with sword and buckler, yet plainly reluctant to use them.

On leaving this superb building there was always plenty to discuss. Why, if it was the shrine of St Wenceslas, was it called after St Vitus? The cathedral was originally founded by St Wenceslas and could not be dedicated to himself, nor was he a saint at the time. Vitus was a Saxon saint, and

Wenceslas was on friendly terms with the Saxon dynasty. The saint always came late to the Imperial councils held by Henry, the Saxon king, until in the end the king was so angry with him that he gave orders that none of the princes should rise and offer their seat to him when he arrived. To everyone's surprise, when he finally came, the king suddenly stood up himself and offered him the place of honour. He explained afterwards that he had been about to rebuke Wenceslas, when he suddenly saw two angels beside him and a blazing cross on his forehead. Wenceslas's helmet, which is kept among the relics of the cathedral museum, has a crucifix on the protective piece covering the forehead. Wenceslas was in such high favour with the Saxon kings that he succeeded in obtaining from them some valuable relics of St Vitus, which he placed in the church he built. So long as the relics of St Vitus were in the hands of the Franks, fortune was on their side, but when the relics were transferred to Saxony, power passed to the Saxon kings. So the Czechs at that time hoped that St Vitus would be a reinforcement for them.

What was once a small round church was rebuilt twice and turned into a cathedral, before it was finally completed in the twentieth century. The Emperor Charles created the Wenceslas crown and decreed that it should be worn at every coronation. The crown jewels were locked away in the Wenceslas chapel and access to the casket in which they were kept was by seven keys. Even as late as under the Nazi occupation during the last war, the Reichsprotektor received from the President the keys of the crown jewels, kept four for himself and returned three to him. The ceremony symbolized the momentary extinction of Czech sovereignty.

During the German occupation the Nazis tried to exploit the historic friendship between St Wenceslas and the Saxon kings to show that the Czech national saint was the first 'collaborator'. As can be imagined this had very little effect on the Czechs. On the contrary, although they had lost much of their historic religious fervour, the people still regarded St Wenceslas as their intercessor. In moments of stress they continued to pray to him and in the words of the ancient chorale – one of the oldest Czech musical compositions – begged him not to let them perish. Though the saint is a legendary figure and not much of his legend has historical foundations, his first biography was written soon enough after his death for there to be contemporaries still alive who could attest whether what was written was true or not. We know from it that he was opposed to capital punishment and prisons, that he helped the poor, that he ransomed slaves from the market place and baptized them and that he was literate (unlike most rulers of his time), reading both Latin and Slav. Is it not a good thing that our Christmas carol, 'Good King Wenceslas', which we have all been taught to sing from our childhood, is about a Czech prince whose ideas were so advanced and humane for his time?

A view of St Vitus' Cathedral from the east circa 1825 by J. Šembera

St Wenceslas statue by Peter Parler (1330–99) in St Vitus' Cathedral

St Vitus' Cathedral in the mid-nineteenth century; engraving by K. Würbs

The bust of Charles IV in St Vitus' Cathedral

Prague in 1493 by A. Schedel

Rudolf II (inset) and the Vladislav Hall (the Old
Royal Palace) by E. Sadeler

The Golden Lane circa 1930; photographer unknown

Sixteenth-century alchemist's laboratory, artist unknown

The Second Prague Defenestration on 23 May 1618, artist unknown

The Thun Palace in the eighteenth century by
M. Engelbrecht and F. Bernhard Werner

St Nicholas Church circa 1820 by S. Prout

A view of the Charles Bridge in the 1840s by F. X. Sandman

A view of the Vltava from the Charles Bridge circa 1810 by A. Pucherna

The Charles Bridge in the nineteenth century

The Charles Bridge in the wake of the 1890 flood; photographer unknown

The Old Royal Palace

[22] In 1212, in an imperial edict, *The Golden Bull of Sicily*, the Holy Roman Emperor Friedrich II confirms the reigning Czech monarch Přemysl Otakar I as a sovereign over lands with the hereditary 'royal dignity of a kingdom', and bestows on the new Czech kingdom special privileges.

Friedrich, by the grace of God elected Roman Emperor, for ever the aggrandizer of the Empire, King of Sicily, Duke of Apulia and Prince of Capons.

Because the ornament and the power of Empire bestows on us the right that from Our Majesty issues the bestowal of the dignity not only of princes but also royal sceptres, We regard it as a glorious and important event that even to others, from the great blessing of Our bounty, we extend the royal dignity without Our supremacy suffering in any way thereby.

Therefore We regard the pre-eminently devoted services which all the Czech People from far off times have faithfully and devotedly shown to the Roman Emperor, and that their obvious King Otakar from the outset especially elected us Emperor in preference to the other princes unceasingly and effectively persevered in our election.

To the perpetual memory and power of this Our decision and confirmation We have recommended this *p r i v i l e g- i u m* to be written by the hand of Henry of Paris, Our faithful notary, and to confirm this by Our gold *B u l l a* of the year, month and indiction written below . . .

This took place in the year of the incarnation of the Lord, one thousand two hundred and twelve on the 26th day of the month of September, in the reign of our Lord Friedrich, the Sublime, elected Roman Emperor, King of Sicily, the fifteenth year. Given at the noble city of Basel by the hand of Oldich, vice-notary, twenty-sixth September, amen.

[23] In 1333 a young Luxembourg prince (the future Holy Roman Emperor and Czech king Charles IV) travels from Italy to Prague where he builds 'a new and beautiful' royal palace; from his autobiography *Vita Caroli.*

After, our father saw that his financial resources were running out and he could not further pursue the war against the lords of Lombardy, he thought about withdrawing, and wanted to give the cities and the war over into our command. We, however, declined, for we were not able to maintain ourselves with honour. He then gave us permission to depart and sent us on to Bohemia. Having received a guarantee of safe passage from our enemies, we crossed through the territory of Mantua to Verona and from there to the county of Tyrol. Then we travelled through Bavaria, where we met our older sister Margaret, who had had only one son with Duke Henry of Bavaria (his name was John).

Eventually we arrived in Bohemia, from which we had been absent for eleven years. There we found that, some years before, our mother Elisabeth had died. While she was alive her second daughter, our sister Guta, had been sent to France to marry John, the first-born son of King Philip of

France, to whose sister Blanche we were married. Our third and last sister, Anne, had been spending this time in France with our aforementioned sister. And thus when we arrived in Bohemia, we found neither father nor mother nor brother nor sisters nor anyone else we knew. In addition, we had completely forgotten the Czech language which we have since relearned so that we speak it and understand it like any other Bohemian. By divine grace therefore we know how to speak, write, and read not only Czech, but French, Italian, German, and Latin so that we are able to write, read, speak, and understand any one of these languages as well as another.

Our father was going to the county of Luxemburg because of a war against the duke of Brabant which he and his comrades were waging together – namely the bishop of Liege, the margrave of Jülich, the count of Geldern, and many, many others – and he transferred authority in Bohemia to us for the duration of his absence.

We found the kingdom so forsaken that there was not one castle which was free and not mortgaged together with all its royal property, so that we did not have anywhere to stay except in houses in the cities just like any other citizen. Even the castle in Prague was desolate, in ruins, and reduced from the times of King Otakar so that it had crumbled almost to the ground. Here we raised up at great expense the great, new, and beautiful palace the way it appears to those who look on it today.

[24] In the mid-fourteenth century the Czech king and Holy Roman Emperor Charles IV, contemplates the beauty of his royal city and its bright future from the balcony of the Royal Palace; from *The Old Czech Legends* by Alois Jirásek, translated by Edith Pargeter, Prague, 1963.

Once Charles the Fourth invited to his castle of Prague Archbishop Arnošt of Pardubice, the high Chancellor, the burgrave of the Czech kingdom and other distinguished Czech lords and courtiers, together with certain masters renowned for their arts, among them his astronomer. He sat down with them in a splendid hall, the wooden ceiling of which was ornamented with carvings, painting and gilding, and its walls covered with rare French tapestries. They sat at a table gleaming with wax candles and shining with gold and silver dishes, plates, goblets and jugs of beautiful form and rich ornamentation.

When they had supped, and it was beginning to be close and sultry in the hall, the emperor rose and invited his guests to go out with him and cool themselves in the fresh air. He went before with the archbishop, leading the way on to a balcony to which their dining room gave immediate access, and after them went the lords and the scholars in lively conversation.

But as they emerged on the spacious balcony the emperor and his counsellor fell silent, and all the others hushed their talk. They stood mute with astonishment at the beauty of the royal city below them.

Prague slumbered in the summer night, in the flooding light of the full moon and in deep shadows. In this enchanted light the gables and roofs of the tall houses, the churches, the towers soared in beauty, the windows of the buildings and the great oriels glittered, and the bushy crowns of the trees in the many gardens and on the islands mingled in the gleaming radiance with soft, cloudy outlines.

And all in deep stillness. Only the weirs below hummed and murmured. King and courtiers, charmed by all this loveliness, stood gazing through light and dark; their eyes wandered along the slopes of Petřín in the blue dimness, over the Little Quarter immediately beneath them; they beheld its illuminated spaces, the archbishop's palace by the river, where the gilded roof of its fortified tower burned; they looked across the modest bridge, along the river, shimmering like spilled silver, and beyond to the rest of Prague, the Jewish Town, the Old Town enclosed in its ramparts and bastions, above which towers and churches soared towards the night sky. There the streets and arcades had grown dark, there all things were drowned in light and shadow and deep twilight.

And they looked beyond the Old Town, along the plateau with its wide spaces, where the church of Saint Lazarus showed white and pale, and the church of Saint Peter on the hill of Zderaz stood freely, not hemmed in by a crowd of houses; where the village of Opatovice drowsed and the church of Saint Stephen in the village of Rybník towered high in the pallid moonlight, and beyond it the church of Saint John on the Battlefield. There the sheen of the moonlight flowed freely over gardens, orchards and fields of ripe grain, far to the horizon, to the heights planted with vineyards, misty with white vapours.

Silent every one, they gazed on this enchanting picture outspread before them, until the king, moved by so much beauty, said:

'Beautiful is this land of mine, and in it I find my greatest delight. I hold it as a chosen and more precious orchard among my other fields. But in this orchard the place of the greatest consolation and joy – behold, Prague! Is there anything more beautiful?'

The king's eyes were shining.

'A most beautiful city,' said Arnošt of Pardubice, 'and most happy, as the chronicler calls it, because it was exalted by a sainted prince. And now it is and will still be adorned by your love. The prophecy of your Majesty's first ancestress is already fulfilled. Prague grows in greatness and glory. Princes bow to her, she enjoys honour and praise throughout the world. And she will be yet more glorious.'

'With the help of God I will gladly adorn her,' said the king sincerely.

'God bless your Majesty!'

As Charles the Fourth had resolved, so he did.

Often the king talked and took counsel with the builder, and often came to see how the work was progressing, and on every occasion he spoke to a mason here or a day – labourer there, questioned them and made them gifts, pleased that the work was continuing successfully.

Only once he grew angry, and that was when he came to look at the New Town on returning from a journey into the German empire, and saw that the surveyors had added a new street in his absence. It led to the church of Saint Henry, and already they were building the houses along it.

As the emperor saw it he stood in amazement and displeasure, and asked sharply who had ordered this street to be founded and laid out there. 'No-one ordered it, your gracious Majesty,' said the builder, dismayed. 'We thought that it would be suitable. But if you wish it to be halted –'.

'Let it remain,' decided the emperor, 'but let it be named for all time Unauthorised, since I gave no order for its establishment.'

So the New Town grew. The buildings increased like mushrooms after rain. But it was not only the citizens of the new city who were building, for the lord of the Czech lands himself built, also. And that most lavishly: monasteries, and towered churches. Thus he founded also the church of Saint Jerome, and beside it the monastery of the Benedictine monks in that region of Skalky, where ages before had flourished the grove of the goddess Morana. He raised this church at great expense. It is said that special tiles were fired for this building, identical with those in the castle of Karlštejn, of grey clay and glazed on the upper surface, and the church roof was designed so thoroughly and artistically that they used for it the tree-trunks from a whole forest.

The church and the monastery were twenty years in the building, and it was an expensive undertaking. It is said that this church cost to build not a penny less than did the Stone Bridge itself.

When it was completed and the first sacred service held in it, the priests at the altar sang in the Slav language, and they read Holy Mass in the ancient ceremony from Slav books, for the first time for centuries in a Czech church.

Then there was joy in the heart of the pious Czech king who had brought these Slavonic monks here from Dalmatia, and all the people rejoiced with him. And they gave to both monastery and church the name of Na Slovanech, the place of the Slavs, and so they are called to this day.

[25] On 23 May 1618, a group of more than 100 Protestant nobles attacks two Catholic governors, Martinic and Slavata, and their secretary Fabricius, and throws them from the windows of the Bohemian Chancellery; from *History of the Church* by Pavel Skála of Zhoře and (2) *Wallenstein* by Francis Watson, London, 1989.

Count Schlick, ardently and with tears in his eyes, for he was a true and zealous follower of the religion, addressed the assembly and violently attacked Martinic and Slavata. He reminded them of the wrongs which they had inflicted . . . on the whole Evangelical Church.

. . . He said that they had unlawfully attempted to deprive the Protestants of their offices, and that they had given proof of this when they deprived that noble Bohemian hero, Count Thurn, of his office as burgrave of the Karlstein, which office Martinic had usurped; he had done this contrary to the constitution of the land. 'But you (Martinic and Slavata),' Count Schlick said, 'worthless disciples of the Jesuits, you with your followers have dared to take it on yourselves to do this, not knowing how otherwise to harm us and to disparage our party. But you shall learn that we are not old women and that we shall not allow you to deceive us. As long as old men, honest and wise, governed this kingdom, everything went well in it; but since you, disciples of the Jesuits, have pushed yourselves forward, the contrary has been the case. You will not be able to take from us the privileges which God has given us and our gracious sovereign has confirmed.' Then Count Thurn quickly approached Slavata and seized him by the hand, while Ulrick Kinsky seized Martinic – but many nobles did not yet know what would be done with them, whether they would be thrown into a dungeon or merely put under arrest; then they (Thurn and Kinsky) led them right through the crowd of nobles; and only then did every one know that they would be thrown from the windows.

. . . They now began to entreat that their lives be spared; wringing their hands and invoking the name of God, they strove to keep their feet on the ground and begged for mercy.

. . . But no mercy was granted them . . . and they were both thrown, dressed in their cloaks and with their rapiers and decorations . . . one after the other head foremost out of the westward window into the moat beneath the palace, which by a wall is separated from the other deeper moat. They loudly screamed and attempted to hold on to the window-frame, but were at last obliged to let go, as they were struck on the hands.

(2) Immediately beneath the windows, however, chance or a partial providence had placed a dung heap. Unwholesome but yielding, it received in safety the hurtling forms of the councillors, and a moment later that of the secretary Fabricius, who apologized as he joined them for coming to rest in a superior position unsuited to his station. Peering from the windows the Protestants were amazed to see their victims scramble to their feet. A couple of shots were fired after them as they fled, and Martinic was slightly grazed. But all three reached temporary safety. And the news reached Vienna. It meant war; war that was to last for thirty years, and spreading far beyond the confines of Bohemia to engulf the whole of Germany.

[26] The seventeenth-century French visitor Charles Patin gets a rare glimpse of the imperial art collection; from *Travels thro' Germany, Bohemia, Swisserland, Holland and other Parts of Europe*, London, 1697.

The King's Palace is at present that of the Emperor, and, in regard of its advantageous Situation, Architecture, and Ornaments, justly deserves the Title of a Royal Pile of Building. M. Mifferoni to whose Custody the Treasure is committed, gave me a sight there (without any manner of exaggeration be it spoken) of the finest Paintings in the World: There were about fifty of Titian, as also a little Room crowded with the works of Raphael Angelo, and four or five spacious Chambers full of Paintings of the highest Value. I cannot call to mind the sight of some empty rooms without Tears in my Eyes, by reason that all the books and medals were kept in 'em. It is the Property of War to spare nothing; and that which none durst attempt by open Force, was at last effected by the Treachery of a private Person, who enrich'd Count Konismarck with these Treasures. I have been informed that this General made a Present of Part of 'em to Queen Christina; and that he caus'd the rest to be convey'd into a Castle which he has in his possession near Bremen.

The South Wing
(The Presidential Suite)

---

[27] Czechoslovakia's first president, T. G. Masaryk, appoints Jože Plečnik to design and supervize architectural renovation of Prague Castle intended to demonstrate the state's liberation from the Habsburgs in 1920; from *Talks with T. G. Masaryk* by Karel Čapek, Connecticut, 1995 and *Prague* by Jana Claverie and Alena Kubová, Paris, 2002.

The President's brief was clearcut: 'Another important aspect of my politics is refurbishing the Castle, by which I mean turning it into a historical monument, the emblem of our once old, now new state and a symbol of both its past and future. *In concerto*, I wish to transform the monarchist Castle into a democratic Castle.'

In 1920, on the advice of Jan Kotěra, who was designing the presidential apartment, Masaryk appointed Jože Plečnik architect for Prague's Hradčany Castle [*he stayed in this post until 1935*].

Plečnik interpreted Masaryk's brief in his own way. He inserted dark paving into the slabs of the first courtyard to create two oblique paths serving new doors, in order to play down the importance of the central door, called the Mathias door, which was a symbol of the popular iconography and elements drawn from classical Greek, Roman and Etruscan sources, which were completely accessible to citizens of the times. Individual qualities still have to go often to Rome to find it. The use Plečnik made of small scale effects was consistent with the philosophy of 'emotional involvement' of the participants in the experience: regional materials, perfect craftsmanship in the execution of detail, the combining of traditional and modern techniques, all of these were signs and symbols that made interpretation easier, and pointed to the architect's desire to get close to the cultural roots of the inhabitants by means of the work he designed. This was an architecture of dialogue and mutual understanding, consequently democratic. The canopy over the entrance to the staircase of the bull in the southeast corner of the third courtyard is thus an allusion to a regional legend and interprets certain features of Greek architecture without imitating them.

The other ambition of Plečnik was to integrate Hradčany into a proper urban design linking the castle and its immediate surroundings with the city at its foot. The image of Acropolis dominating the Athens skyline, built in the golden age of Greek democracy, was a powerful precedent.

[28] President Edvard Beneš and the Munich Crisis (September/October 1938); from *They Betrayed Czechoslovakia* by G. J. George, London, 1938 and *Guilty Men* by 'Cato', London, 1940.

President Beneš stepped to the window of his study, from which he had a glorious view over the city of a hundred towers lying in the valley far below. A slight haze lay over the spires and roofs. The glorious view that met his eye had in it, as always, a touch of melancholy.

Was this lovely town to be reduced in a few days to a heap of ruins? The German bombers would not spare the glorious monuments of architecture, once they had their orders to begin. But the President was optimistic. He still hoped that even now, at the eleventh hour, the appalling catastrophe might be averted. He firmly believed that if the [*Western*] Powers stood firm, Hitler would abandon his bluff. Dr Beneš is a disciple of the French philosophers, he clung to the philosophy of clear logic and its unbending laws. He was therefore convinced that Germany would not risk a war against overwhelming odds. He forgot that in the Europe of to-day the laws of logic appear to have lost their validity. Feelings and emotions have routed logic.

The President lingered long at his window. He thought on the past and on the Future. The Czechs had been only a mere twenty years in control. Before that, for 300 years, they had been ruled by the Germans of the Habsburg Empire. It was no cause for wonder that here and there old resentments had asserted themselves, and found vent in petty intrigues against which the President could do little, even if he came to know of them. The State was a democratic Republic, and the democratic-bureaucratic machine works slowly. Besides, what are twenty years in the life of a State?

If Czechoslovakia were given time, Germans and Czechs could contrive to live and work together in friendship, to the advantage of both nations. It was no accident that in this Bohemian land Czechs and Germans had lived together for ten centuries. The existence of Bohemia was economically and politically necessary to Europe.

And now it seemed too late. The Czechs had denied autonomy to the Germans because they feared that they would use it to create a totalitarian State within the democratic framework of the Republic. Would a wise compromise still be possible even now, if Germany should give way? President Beneš optimistically believed that even yet a peaceful settlement might be found for the Sudeten Germans within the Czechoslovak Republic.

At this point in his reflections – 6.45 p.m. – his secretary entered. The French and British Ministers requested an audience.

The President granted it.

This time the French Minister spoke first. He spoke solemnly and with profound emotion: 'The French Government', he said, 'have commissioned me to inform Your Excellency that they no longer regard as binding on Czechoslovakia the promise she made not to take extraordinary measures in the present crisis. She is again free to take all steps she thinks imperative for her own safety.'

'His Majesty's Government associates itself unreservedly with this declaration', added the British Minister.

The President replied as calmly as he could,

'Thank you, gentlemen. We shall promptly inform you of whatever measures we take.'

The President knew at once what the Franco-British message implied. The Western Powers considered that the Godesberg negotiations had broken down, and were preparing for the worst. They were now giving Czechoslovakia a free hand.

A council of Cabinet Ministers was summoned at once, and attended also by the Members of the Ministry of Defence and the Generals of the General Staff.

At twenty minutes past 10 that same Friday evening the Czech wireless broadcast the order for mobilization.

By eleven o'clock Prague lay in complete darkness. The first attack of the German air force was expected.

On Sunday, October 2, 1938, the German tanks and troops advanced unopposed across the Czech frontier to take over their new territory (which included, intact, all the fortifications and gun emplacements the Czechs had bled themselves to erect on this German frontier during the previous five years).

On that same Sunday this prayer was ordered to be read in all Catholic Churches by the Roman Catholic Cardinal, Primate of Bohemia.

The land of St Wenceslas has just been invaded by foreign armies and the thousand-year-old frontier has been violated. This sacrifice has been imposed on the nation of St Wenceslas by our ally, France, and our friend, Britain. The Primate of the ancient Kingdom of Bohemia is praying to God Almighty that the peace efforts prompting this terrible sacrifice will be crowned by permanent success and, should they not, he is praying to the Almighty to forgive all those who impose this injustice on the people of Czechoslovakia.

In the Protestant churches of Czechoslovakia the same prayer was offered with the substitution of the name 'John Hus' for 'Saint Wenceslas'.

[29] In 1948, a group of Czech and Slovak sportsmen are invited to Prague Castle to meet Klement Gottwald, the country's 'first workers' president' and the leader of the 'Victorious February' Communist coup which took place earlier that year; from *Zátopek: The Marathon Victor* by František Kožík, translated by Jean Layton, Prague, 1954.

The first year of the reorganization of physical training had brought great progress. President Gottwald was to show his appreciation of the successes of the past season at a special meeting at the Castle.

A specially-selected group of the most successful sportsmen were given the honour of representing the great mass of gymnasts and athletes at this meeting with the head of state.

To-day, through the Matthew [*Matyáš*] Gate, through which usually only the most important visitors, such as diplomats, representatives of foreign lands, are permitted to enter, there strides a group of men and women all bursting with health and energy. They have successfully represented their country at the greatest sports festival in the world, the Olympic Games. One of them is Emil Zátopek.

The President is already waiting for the sportsmen. After they have been introduced to him, he thanks them for their splendid services. From his words one can tell how interested he is in sport and how well informed he is on everything to do with sport. As a young man he had also been a gymnast in the Worker's Sports Union.

'I think that the latest events in our physical training and sports life clearly show that we are taking the right road.

We want this important factor in our public life to be both a pleasure and a relaxation for our people so that they will gather sufficient strength for the construction and defence of our beautiful homeland.'

And he did not forget to add that much importance was attached to the performances of the outstanding experts in the various fields.

'Therefore, dear friends, may the broadest masses of the people participate in physical culture and forward to the conquest of new records and championships!' With elated spirits, the select group sat in a circle round the President and discussed all the problems which interested or worried them: the question of new stadiums, sportsgrounds, gymnasiums, the training of instructors, the training methods of the outstanding athletes, the education of the youth through the clubs and schools.

Concluding the discussion Emil Zátopek said the following:

'In the name of all our sportsmen I want to thank you for the fact that with the liberation of our people you have also given physical education a new meaning. Thanks to this great achievement, our whole nation can now participate in physical training and our leading sportsmen can go forward to the finest performances. It is a great honour for us to be able to defend our country's flag beyond the borders. We do so out of gratitude to our fatherland.'

Emil stood there smartly in front of his supreme commander. President Klement Gottwald shook him cordially by the hand and recalled how often he had crossed his fingers for Emil, how much he would have wished him the honour of the Olympic victory over the 5,000 metres.

Very moved and with added confidence the sportsmen left the Castle.

The Golden Lane

[30] When the Habsburg Emperor Rudolf II moved his court from Vienna to Prague in 1583, the city became an academy of the occult. Like 'gnats to sweet wine' magicians, astrologers and alchemists flocked to Prague from all over Europe; from *Magic Prague* by Angelo Maria Ripellino translated by David Newton Marinelli, London, 1994.

In the hope of replenishing coffers drained by the acquisition of so many rarities and of obtaining an elixir to prolong his life, Rudolf surrounded himself with a crowd of eccentric distillers, whom he extolled and showered with gifts only to throw them into a cramped cell once they disappointed him.

The luted vessels, the flasks, the hermaphrodites, perturbations and marriages, the coupling of elements, the katabasis into infernal regions, the coitus of King Sulphur and Queen Mercury for the generation of philosopher's gold, the oneness of the sufferings of metals in the alembics and the passion of Our Lord, the gripe's egg, the glass spheres, the hollow trees, symbol of the athanor – all this alchemical magic kept Rudolf from affairs of state and stirred his imagination to a frenzied pitch.

Alchemy fits perfectly into Rudolf's world and its predilection for the occult, for Mannerist freaks, hybrids, curiosities, composites and clay androids.

The agents Rudolf set loose in foreign lands in search of *objets d'art* also had a mandate to track down alchemists and entice them to his court with gifts and promises. For the charlatans – who travelled the length and breadth of Europe – Bohemia was something of a California of the spagyric art.

Tradition has it that the alchemists of the Rudolfine era lived in the tiny houses of Golden Lane (*Zlatá ulička*), a dreamy, lilliputian street on the periphery of the opulent Castle. [*Gustav*] Meyrink, who according to Max Brod [*Kafka's biographer*] had himself sought the philosophers' stone, gives this description of it:

'A narrow, winding lane with crenels, a snail's path barely wide enough for one's shoulders to pass. I am standing in front of a row of small houses, none of which is taller than myself. Were I to stretch out my arm I could touch the roofs. Here during the Middle Ages disciples set the philosophers' stone aglow and poisoned moon beams.'

Oskar Wiener writes:

> It is actually a cheerful street that looks as though it had been built from a toy-box. The bright doll's houses, the largest of which is hardly more than four square paces, are stuck against the wall enclosing the Stag Moat. Although the queer little cul-de- sac is currently inhabited by the poor, the tiny rooms, each of which constitutes a house in itself, are kept scrupulously clean, and geraniums and carnations blossom in the windows, of which there are never more than two.

According to legend, Rudolf, who was suspicious by nature, kept a close eye on his long-haired alchemists in Golden Lane. Each of them received a *Puppenhaus* as a home and laboratory and was required to wait around the clock for transmutations. A *Landsknecht* with a halbert patrolled the little street night and day.

. . . The legend claiming that the alchemists resided in Golden Lane goes back . . . to the late Romantic period. In fact, Golden Lane came into being during Rudolf's reign because the Castle, a city within a city, was not subject to the laws governing the rest of Prague, and a rabble of shop-keepers, unregistered craftsmen, pedlars and persons of ill repute took refuge within its walls. The row of toy houses grew up alongside the Stag Moat – clinging to the complex organism of the Castle like a parasite – with the tacit consent of the authorities. The street's name came from the fact that there were goldsmiths among the original inhabit-ants, but archers, Castle guards and gaolers also made their homes here. Craftsmen, merchants and even archers amassed considerable profits from selling provisions, bev-erages and objects of use to the prisoners in the two towers that delimit the Lane: the White Tower, where alchemists were often incarcerated, and the Daliborka [*dungeon*].

. . . The latter took its name from the knight Dalibor z Kozojed, who was imprisoned there at the end of the fifteenth century for supporting the peasants of the Litoměřice region in their revolt against a cruel squire. Fearing that the solitude and endless silence in the remote dungeon, from which he could not see so much as a patch of sky, would drive him mad, Dalibor had a violin brought him, and practised so much that he attracted the curious from all over Prague. In spring the prisoner's sad trills competed with the birds chirping in the Stag Moat, nor did the violin cease its sobbing until Dalibor died beneath the executioner's axe in 1498. Every legend is to some extent based on fact, and in fact the heartrending music was none other than the cries of Dalibor being tortured on the rack or 'violin' in hangman's jargon. Which of course does not prevent him from playing in the haunted tower on moonlit nights.

Even if the belief that there were alchemists among the tenants of Golden Lane may stem from the fact that its tiny houses were inhabited by goldsmiths, the historical expla-nation is no less fascinating than the legend, because it pro-vides us with a Kafkaesque picture of a parasitic world at the perimeter of a mysterious Castle.

. . . Of course, no one can erase the legendary connection between the alchemists and the small, narrow street. We can say along with [*the Czech poet*] Nezval:

> In the Golden Lane in the Hradčany
> time almost seems to stand still
> If you wish to live five hundred years
> drop everything take up alchemy
>
> When that simple miracle comes to be
> our rivers will exhale their gold
> Farewell farewell charlatan say hello
> for us to the coming century

. . . The Golden Lane, then, though a scanty architectural complex that seems conjured by a magic wand, acts as the backdrop for the dramatic miracle of transmutation. Much of the demonic nature of the city on the Vltava emanates from its houses. In Karásek's drama *Král Rudolf* . . . [*the astrologer Dr*] Dee confesses:

I love wondrous Prague, which is as unique and enchanting as its melancholy king. Believe me, this gloomy city plants a glow of madness in the brain of those who make it their own. The Golden Lane, where Rudolf has placed his alchemists' forges, is the city's soul. So much energy, so much magnetism of occult forces is concentrated there that experiments which fail elsewhere will succeed there.

To complete the picture we must mention the fact that the Polish writer Stanislaw Przybyszewski, idol of the Czech decadents, was unsuccessful in his efforts to settle in Golden Lane and that the renowned Prague fortune-teller Madame de Thèbes lived in one of the houses – number 4 – before the Second World War. Three worn-out cards, three cards on the heavy tablecloth, many yellowed photographs on the walls and a magnificent view of the Stag Moat. As in the dark fortune-teller's booths in Josefov, a plump tomcat with a belly like a drum prowling the small room when not curled up, like Beardsley's black cat, in his mistress's basket-like coiffure.

[31] In 1916, Franz Kafka moves temporarily into this little street, at No 22; from *The Biography of Franz Kafka* by Max Brod, London, translated by G. Humphreys Roberts, London, 1947.

In the winter of 1916–17, Franz lived in the Alchemists' Street. Legends are already growing up around the place where he stayed, and foreigners who come to Prague are shown the tiny little house and the room that 'the author' used to live in – they are almost identical. The house consists of only the one room, together with a tiny kitchen and a loft. But Franz didn't choose this quarter at all from any mystic or romantic inclination, or at least any such inclination was not the deciding factor, except perhaps subconsciously, in the form of an old love for old Prague; in the foreground was Franz's need for a quiet place to work in. His extraordinarily keen sensitivity to noise, with which he even occasionally infected me, by suggestion – when we travelled together, for example – made the choice difficult. In the Alchemists' Street Franz felt comparatively happy, and was extremely grateful to his youngest sister who had discovered this refuge for him – as she did later in Zürau.

On 11 February 1917, a Sunday, I wrote, 'With Kafka in the Alchemists' Street. He read aloud beautifully. The monastic cell of a real writer.'

. . . Franz had his own personal mysticism; he couldn't take over from others a ready-made ritual. He was often alone, and enjoyed being alone. The 'most beautiful place in Prague' was the description he gave of the Chotek gardens, where he used to go again and again for lonely walks. 'The birds were singing, the castle with its gallery, the ancient trees, with last year's leaves still hanging on them, the semi-darkness.'

The Royal Summer Palace

[32] The famous Elizabethan mathematician and astrologer Dr John Dee (who coined the term 'the British Empire'), and his companion, alchemist Edward Kelley, arrive for an audience with Emperor Rudolf II in his summer palace (the Belvedere) adjoining Prague Castle; from *The Angel of the West Window* by Gustav Mayrink, London, 1991.

Hradčany Castle towers above the city with bristling defenses; every gateway echoes with the jingle of spurs, the clash of ever-ready weapons. We ride slowly up the hill. Suspicious eyes follow us from the tiny windows above. Three times already have we been unexpectedly stopped by guards who suddenly appear from nowhere to ask us our business. The emperor's letter granting us audience is checked again and again. Then we are out on the splendid approach, the city of Prague spread out below us. I look at the view like a prisoner gazing out on the free world. Up here everything seems to be in the tight grip of an invisible hand. Up here the summit of the hill has become a prison!

The city below seems to lie in a sea of silver dust. Above us the sun smoulders through a misty veil. The bell of the high-vaulted cathedral of St Nicholas below strikes ten; from somewhere within the ramparts of the stronghold in front of us a sharp, imperative clock repeats the hour with a swift drumroll – it is high time! . . .

We have reached the top and could set our steeds at a gallop were it not for the halberdiers that block our every step; there is no end to the checks and scrutiny. Finally the bridge over the deer moat [*Stag Moat*] thunders beneath our horses' hooves, and we are trotting across the quiet park of the hermit king.

Surrounded by ancient oaks, the green copper roof of the airy Belvedere rises before us like a huge upturned ship's hull. We jump from our horses.

The first thing to attract my eye are stone reliefs on the balustrade of the loggia formed by delicate arches around the Belvedere. There is Samson wrestling with the lion and, opposite, Hercules overcoming the Nemean lion. They are the symbols that the emperor chooses to guard the entrance to his ultimate refuge. It is well known that the lion is his favourite animal and that he has trained a huge African lion as a pet with which he likes to frighten even his intimates. All around it is deserted and silent. No one to receive us?! A bell with a note like a crystal goblet sounds the quarter. Clocks even here!

At the last stroke plain wooden door opens. Wordlessly, a gray-haired servant invites us to enter. Stable boys suddenly appear to take our horses. We are standing in the long, cool hall of the Belvedere Palace. The stench of camphor is suffocating. The whole room is piled high with glass cases full of strange, exotic specimens: life-size models of savages in bizarre poses going about their bizarre business, weapons, gigantic animals, all kinds of implements, Chinese flags, Indian totem poles, an abundance of curiosities from the Old and the New World. At a sign from our guide we stop beside the immense nightmare figure of a shaggy wood wight with a satanically grinning skull. Kelly's bravura has withdrawn to the inmost recesses of his fur. He whispers some nonsense about evil spirits. I have to smile at the mountebank who does not tremble at all before his own conscience, but cowers in fear of a stuffed gorilla.

But at that very same moment I feel my bowels gripped with a shock of fear as a black ghost floats soundlessly around the corner beyond the ape's case and a scrawny figure faces us. Yellow hands pull a shabby black gown tight around him and fidget under the folds with a weapon. The outline of a short dagger is clear to see. A pale birdlike head is lit by yellow eagle's eyes. The emperor!

[33] John Dee and Edward Kelley attend an audience with Emperor Rudolf II; from *John Dee; Scientist, Geographer & Secret Agent to Elizabeth I*, by Richard Deacon, London, 1968.

On 3 September, Dee and Kelley, having left their wives and Dee's family behind in Cracow, were received by Rudolf [*sic*] in Prague. The interview was friendly, though the Emperor seemed to take a dislike to Kelley and gave nearly all his attention to Dee. He said he had heard of Dee's fame from the Spanish Ambassador in Prague and commended him on the erudition of his book, *Monad* but added that it was beyond his capacity to understand and stressing somewhat cynically that Dee should confine his attentions only to those things which would be useful to the Emperor. Dee took no notice of this very plain hint and proceeded to harangue Rudolf on the philosophic purpose of his 'angelic conversations'. It must have been a strange meeting, with a bored Emperor listening moodily to a long tirade and Dee declaiming like a preacher of woe and sparing no punches in telling Rudolf some unpleasant truths about himself.

'The Angel of the Lord has appeared to me,' said Dee, 'and rebuketh you for your sins. If you will hear me and believe me, you shall triumph. If you will not hear me, the Lord, the God that made Heaven and Earth (under whom you breathe and have your spirit) putteth down his foot against your breast and will throw you headlong down from your seat. Moreover the Lord has made this covenant with me (by oath) that He will do and perform.

'If you will forsake your wickedness and turn unto Him, your seat shall be the greatest there ever was and the Devil shall become your prisoner.'

It was, whatever way one looks at it, either a very valiant, or an extremely impertinent performance on Dee's part, but there can be no denying that it must have required a good deal of courage to berate the Emperor for his sins in his own palace. But though Dee's speech was the thunder and lightning of declamatory prose, he was calm, courteous and even deferential. There was nothing of the uncouthness of John Knox's tirade against Mary, Queen of Scots, in this spontaneous recital by Dee. But it was not an auspicious beginning to their association and Rudolf, an eccentric and erratic man, was no doubt at least irritated by it, if not downright angered, though he seems to have kept his feelings to himself and to have made a civil enough reply. But he committed himself to nothing and when Dee went on to speak of his 'angelic conversations', he urged him to defer this until a later date, saying, according to Dee, that 'he would henceforward take me to his recommendation and care, and some such words (of favour promised) which I heard not well, he spake so low.'

No doubt Rudolf was exhausted by this time and probably Dee, ever an optimist, mistook the inaudible tones for a note of encouragement which Rudolf was far from conceding. When Dee sought a further interview he was told that the Emperor was away hunting and that in future all communications with him must be made through an intermediary, Dr Kurtz, a member of his Council. It was in effect a polite dismissal.

Dee, unabashed and refusing to be discouraged, did his best to influence Dr Kurtz and the Spanish Ambassador, but without achieving any worthwhile result. On 28 September he sent the Emperor a letter, saying that it was at the command of the spirits and claiming that he had found the 'Philosopher's Stone'.

This was followed by another communication to the Spanish Ambassador stating that he had 'progressed in incredible mysteries' which he was preparing to reveal to the Emperor alone.

In Prague Dee stayed in the house of a Dr Hageck, 'near the old Rathaus, the greate clock tower'. He and Kelley were joined by Kelley's brother, Thomas, and Edmond Hilton, and shortly after this Dee noted in his diary that 'Satan is very busy with E.K.'

Yet another son was born to Dee at this time and he was given the name of Michael, after the Great Archangel, being baptized in Prague Cathedral when Mrs Dee was well enough to travel again.

Dee tried hard to interest Dr Kurtz in his astronomical research, telling him of the 'battering glass' he had contrived for taking observations on dark nights. But neither promises of the intellectual benefits which the angels could bestow on him, nor the hints that the powder of projection could produce gold moved Rudolf to any real interest in Dee or Kelley. The Emperor told Dr Kurtz that he would require positive proof before he could even consider the possibility of gold being manufactured. Dee and Kelley at this time lacked laboratory equipment and Rudolf declined to assist them. The travellers from England were again short of money and even Jane Dee was moved to make a petition of her own to the angels. Dee noted in his diary in the early part of 1585 that 'My wife, being in great perplexity, requested E.K. and me that the annexed petition might be propounded to God and his good angels to give answer.' Jane's 'petition', or prayer, is still among Dee's manuscripts in the British Museum and it reads:

We desire, God, of his greate and infinite mercies to grant us the helpe of His hevenly mynisters, that we may by them be directed how or by whom to be ayded and released in this necessitie for meate and drinke for us and for our familie, wherewith we stand at this instant much oppressed: and the rather because it might be hurtful to us and the credit of the actions wherein we are linked and vowed unto His hevenly

Majestie (by the mynistry and comfort of His holy angels) to lay such thinges as are the ornament and our house and the coveringe of our bodies in pawne, either unto such as are rebels agaynst his Divine Majestie, the Jewes, or the people of this cytteye, which are malicious and full of wicked slander – I, Jane Dee, humbly acknowledging myselfe His servant and hand-mayden to whom I commit my body and sowle.
'Edward Kelley wrote this for Jane Dee.'

This may have been an attempt on Kelley's part to induce Jane Dee to support the principle of the seances, but from all we know of Jane she must have been desperate indeed to lend herself to any scheme of Kelley's.

[34] Emperor Rudolf's court painter Arcimboldo paints fantastic images made up of objects such as fruits, flowers and animals; from *Magic Prague* by Angelo Maria Ripellino, translated by David Newton Marinelli, London, 1994.

Giuseppe Arcimboldo (1527–93), 'the most ingenious of fantastic painters' followed Rudolf II to Prague, where he became so integral a part of the atmosphere at court that he was identified with the mythology of the period, taking on something of the magical ambivalence and saturnine melancholy characteristic of the alchemists.

Arcimboldo's art, then, is closely linked to Rudolf's preferences: his love of *Automaten* (mechanical dolls and artificial men like the Golem), his alchemistic sense for the amalgam of disparate bodies and especially his collection mania. There is an intimate relationship between Arcimboldo's mixed portraits and Rudolf's *Kunstkammer*, a cabinet of naturalia, rarities and anomalies. Arcimboldo's figures are themselves collections, agglomerations of objects, fruits, flowers and animals. It is no accident that Arcimboldo as an old man continued to acquire 'curiosities' for Rudolf's great museum.

The Four Seasons, for example, is a veritable stockpile of vegetal elements. *Summer* (1563): a profile of fruits and vegetables with grapes for teeth, a pear for a chin, the cheek an apple, the nose a cucumber, the ear an ear of corn and the hair a luxuriant still life. The choice of fruits and vegetables for the parts of the head is so ingenious that the astonishment one feels must approach wonder.

Arcimboldo's passion for curiosities goes hand in hand with the feeling for detail characteristic of many painters at Rudolf's court. Bartolomdus Spranger, Pieter Stevens and Roelant Savery lavished attention on every hair, every branch, every stem, every pebble in their landscapes, menageries and 'nature manuals'. Arcimboldo uses animals as allegories of character defects, passions and the dismantling of the spirit. All the animals constituting the head of *Earth* have allegorical meaning.

. . . It is no simple matter to find one's way in this dense cluster, in this intarsia of animals, in this interlacing of ears, tails, hooves and horns that makes *Earth* into a kind of Noah's Ark, a bestiary similar to the landscapes of Roelant Savery, these oppressive jumbles of turkey-cocks, baboons, amphibians, stags, birds and wild beasts. From the back of the neck to the brow the head is all monkey, ibex, horse, wild boar, bear, mule, stag, deer, leopard, gazelle, dog, camel and lion. The fox, 'slyest of animals', is the brow, its tail the eyebrows. The ear and cheek are a bashful oliphant supported by a donkey. The rabbit, unwary but with an excellent sense of smell, forms the round nose with its back.

The Černín Palace

[35] In 1947 the British diplomat Sir Robert Bruce Lockhart stays as a guest of Jan Masaryk in the Černín Palace – then as now, the Ministry of Foreign Affairs. On the 10 March 1948, Jan Masaryk was found dead in the courtyard of the building after a fall from his top floor flat; from *The Diaries of Sir Robert Bruce Lockhart*, London, 1980.

Saturday, 17 May 1947

Jan threw a party for me tonight and opened his reception rooms . . .

Marvellous food: ham galore, wonderful salads, *hors d'oeuvre*, chicken etc., vodka, slivovice, white wine, whisky, beer, cognac.

Great thing was to get Jan to play the piano, which he apparently does very rarely now, and everyone relied on me. It took a long time – and a fair amount of vodka – to bring him to the stool, but when he began he went on for hours. Madame Hurban, who must have had a fine voice, and he sang various Czech songs – all very plaintive and in the Slav minor keys. Better music than the Russian gypsy songs. I must study them. Jan was very sentimental, and his eyes filled with tears as he sang.

He is most attractive in his sudden changes of moods. He can switch from tears to ribaldry and back again in a few seconds. In one sense his best performance was his imitation of Prokofiev who has been here for the music festival. Jan plays and improvises well enough to take off almost anybody, and he started with a magnificent series of discordant chords in the bass with a kind of bird twittering in the treble with his right hand. Then he switched to melody, [*he*] said: 'Now a little melody,' played a few bars, then he looked very frightened, raised his left hand, bit his finger, whispered: 'No, no, Stalin doesn't allow it,' then with both hands crashed into a finale of discordant chords. It was brilliant.

Tuesday, 20 May 1947

I stayed with Jan at the Czernin [*sic*] Palace and saw more of him during my six days in Prague than in all the thirty years that I have known him. I had a superb suite with vast bathroom, dressing-room, sitting-room, and a bedroom with a superb view over the Hradčany and the whole city. I was waited on hand and foot. Jan gave me much of his time. I had several meals alone with him, and every night at the end of our work we sat up for an hour and had a talk over the present and the past.

Politically he is much happier than he was. He does not really like the Russians and is still afraid of them, especially if there is no understanding between the USSR and the US. He is also irritated by the attitude of the US who do not wish to give loans to countries which have Communists in the government. He can understand their refusing money to entirely totalitarian countries; but to refuse money to, or impose conditions on, a country like Czechoslovakia where the non-Communist parties are making head-way against the Communists is playing into the hands of the latter. He is, however, more or less reassured that Czechoslovakia is out of the wood and quite certain that the Communists are on the down-grade and very much on the defensive.

Physically he is a tired man with strong streak of melancholia in his character. He lives on his nerves – and they are highly strung. I have never seen any man so jumpy as he was before his Tábor speech; yet when he was at the rostrum he seemed as calm and collected as a cricket umpire. His reactions are rapid in their variability. He can be very serious. No one can play the comedian-politician more effectively. He can descend with almost repulsive speed from the sublime to the bawdy.

His chief fault as a politician is his inability to say no. He makes more promises than any man can fulfil. He does his best to keep them, but the day is not long enough for all to benefit. It starts on the telephone in his bedroom at 8 a.m. Sometimes he is kept so busy that he cannot get dressed before 11 a.m. The round goes on all day. The result is that he is always tired and after luncheon tries, like Winston, to steal an hour or two in bed. His doctor (Klinger) gave him an overhaul when I was there, and the result, Jan told me, was completely satisfactory.

But whatever the doctor said I know that not only is he tired but that he has a terrible catarrhal cough in the mornings. I have seen him, too, undress – when he was tinged with melancholy – and say in all sincerity: 'I wish to God I could be rid of it all.'

Although he likes his whisky and soda and makes a patent cocktail of his own – slivovice and vermouth mixed – he is not a drinker and, when alone, drinks only beer. He told me, however, that many of his forebears had died of drink and that his grandfather, the old Slovak coachman and father of the President, had been a roaring drunkard.

He may be one hundred per cent physically fit, but I should say that he was suffering from nervous exhaustion if ever a man was. Now that I have seen him at close quarters, I can realize why Beneš fears that melancholic tendency and the mad streak in the Masaryk family.

Why then does he carry on? I am quite sure that he carries on because he feels that it is his duty to his country and to his father. He did not want to go to Tábor, was relieved and pleased when it was over, and was delighted when I told him in all sincerity that he had made a wonderful job of a task that wanted doing.

Equally I believe that today when he has become a great public figure on the international stage, he would find it hard to leave the scene and would be unhappy if he did. He is *not* an office man. He belongs to the public, and whoever belongs to the public can never leave them with impunity.

Yet almost our last conversation was about Winston whom Jan loves and to whom he is so grateful that recently at a big Communist meeting in the Lucerna [*Hall*] in Prague he declared: 'I may not agree with the policy of Mr Churchill today, but I say here and now that for the winning of the war and for our liberation we owe more to Winston Churchill than to any man living' – and was cheered to the echo by the Communists.

[*Lockhart returned to England at the end of May 1947.*]

THE LITTLE
QUARTER

Around Nerudova Street

[36] A seventeenth-century French visitor describes the 'Little Quarter' or the 'Lesser Side' as it is sometimes called; from *Travels thro' Germany, Bohemia, Swisserland, Holland and other Parts of Europe* by Charles Patin, London, 1697.

That part of the City which is situated beyond the River, and commonly call'd the Lesser Side, is much more delightful and scarce anything else is to be seen there but sumptuous Palaces, which amount to the number of above Three hundred; so that this Quarter may well be styl'd the Magazine of the Riches of Bohemia, and of his Imperial Majesty's Hereditary Countries.

[37] Jan Neruda, a nineteenth-century Czech journalist, poet and short story writer captures the spirit of the picturesque quarter and its inhabitants in 1886; from *What Shall We Do With It?* translated by Michael Henry Heim, Prague, 1995.

Have you ever been in the street in the early morning, gentle reader? Not that I wish to insult you. I know that my readers *are* in fact gentle and have no need to rise before nine, but if, say, by chance. And if chance has lured you out of the house earlier than usual, surely you have been keen-sighted enough to observe that one finds things as well as people not otherwise seen there, and keen-witted enough to give some thought to those things and people, but primarily to the things: an old jug standing in front of a house, a milk can wound round with wire at the edge of the pavement, a baking pan in the middle of the road. How did they get there? Did they escape from unguarded shelves and then fail to find their way back home in the light of dawn? Or did they lose their cook during her morning rounds and decide to wait there like a well-trained dog which, having strayed from its master, will sit itself down even in the middle of the road and look this way and that until it is recovered?

Anyway, there is much talk nowadays about cholera – I beg the gentle reader to refrain from interrupting and inquiring after the connection with what has gone before, that is, to let me go on writing as I please, for in the end he shall see that I am less frivolous than he imagines. To repeat, there is much talk about cholera. About the ways one can go about preventing it. Mainly, the fact that keeping one's flat clean is half the battle. Though keeping the air disinfected is also half the battle. As is eating fresh, healthy beef, veal, and pork. And drinking good Pilsener beer. *Summa summarum* if one observes all the regulations, one is two and a half battles ahead of the game, that is, two and a half times healthier than necessary. And why not observe the regulations, when a) they have one's health at heart and b) following official regulations fills one with ineffable delight!

Thus, the moment I read the municipal decree posted on the nearest corner, I turned on my heel and went home. Well, well, I said to myself, the place is actually quite clean. The furniture and floor are under the careful constant care of my Anča; the books are under my own care, true, but a little dust never hurt a book – they even look ostentatious, overbearing, and silly when dusted. As for everything else, well, there isn't really anything else. Just the bed, and what could be cleaner than a bachelor's bed: pillows like two swans, a cover like a field of lilies, a sheet white as snow, a mattress puffy as a bun, a mattress stuffed with straw, with straw. . . .

'Anča!'

'Yes, sir?'

'When did I last change the straw in my mattress?'

'Can't say as I know. Not as long as I've been with you. Must be like sawdust by now.'

Anča has been with me for six years. And when I try to think farther back, I draw a blank. I must have bought it, stuffed and stitched, while still in the blush of youth.

'Anča!'

'Yes, sir?'

'Here are seventy-five kreutzers. Go and buy me three trusses of straw. This very moment!'

Off she flies. She is back in no time dragging three trusses of straw. She grabs the mattress, undoes the stitching, and is about to start stuffing it when she freezes and says, 'What do we do with the old straw?'

Women do have faster minds than men. It would have taken me forever to think of it! Of course. Before we put in the new straw, we have to remove the old, and – what shall we do with it? Toss it out of the window, on somebody's head?

'What do people *do* with old straw?'

'Can't say as I know.'

'Hm,' I say. 'Here are six more kreutzers. Go over to the big house with the rubbish pit. Give the money to the care-taker, and he'll let you empty the straw into the pit.' So men's minds are worth something after all!

Off she goes and back she comes. He won't let her, she says. The servant girls throw hot ashes into the pit and the straw might catch fire. Besides, the pit is almost full and the peasant who empties it is busy and can't come till winter.

'Then what shall we do?'

'Can't say as I know.'

'Well. I know!' I cry out after a bit. The male mind is amazingly fertile.

'Tomorrow is Wednesday, and Wednesday is rubbish day. Take the six kreutzers and give half to the rubbish man and half to the driver. They'll load it onto the cart.'

'Fine, but what will your honour sleep on? I can't put the mattress back on the bed. The stitching's open. The straw would fall through the boards.'

'True. So I'll . . . then I'll . . . I'll just have to sleep on the floor. We'll take the long cushion off the sofa and lay it on the floor, make it up like a bed, and it will be superb. I'll sleep like a king.'

And sleep like a king I did.

Next morning Anča dragged the mattress into the corridor and we waited. As soon as the rubbish man appeared, I leaned out of the window to witness the procedure. Up rattled the cart; out flew Anča with the mattress.

'I couldn't take it even if you gave me a gulden,' he said, giving the horses the whip. 'It's strictly forbidden.'

'This *is* getting ridiculous,' I said. 'It is ridiculous,' she confirmed.

'Well then, come up with something, why don't you! Find out what other people do.'

Off she flew. Within an hour she was back. 'People say the thing to do is to burn it in the stove.'

'Why, of course. How is it we didn't think of that? You know what? Find out whether anyone in the house needs a hot oven for making buns. Or wants to temper his stove. See what I mean?'

Off she flew once more. But no, no one was planning to make buns, no one needed a stove tempered. And she'd better be off to the market. She'd have no time to tend to the straw until evening. She couldn't sit around all day now, could she?

Well, so be it.

What else is there to say? I had a good night's sleep, and next morning Anča and I took the mattress down to the milkwoman. (Anča had made certain she would accept the gift.) It was a splendid moment. When the milkwoman handed me the empty mattress, I was so moved I kissed her hand and embraced her mare and set off for home with moist eyes.

Once there, we stuffed the mattress with the fresh straw, and when it was full I took hold of Anča and started whistling 'O'er the Fresh Green Meadowland,' and we stomped round the mattress till our heads spun.

[38] A British diplomat admires the buildings along the narrow, winding streets of Malá Strana converging on the Castle, in 1934; from *A Time of Gifts* by Patrick Leigh Fermor, London, 1977.

I climb about the steep city in retrospect and rediscover fragments one by one. There are renaissance buildings, light arcaded pavilions and loggias on slim Ionic pillars that could have alighted here from Tuscany or Latinum, but the palaces on the squares and the citadel and the steep wooded slopes belong to the Habsburg afternoon. Troops of Corynthian pillars parade along half-facades of ashlars rusticated like the nail-head patterns on decanters, and symbols and panoplies overflow the pediments. Branching under procession of statues, shallow staircases unite before great doorways where muscle-bound Atlantes strain under the weight of the lintels, and the gardens underneath them are flocked by marble populations. Nymphs bind their collapsing sheaves, goddesses tilt cornucopias, satyrs give chase, nymphs flee, and tritons blow fanfares from their twirling shells . . .

Terraces climb the hillside in a giant staircase and somewhere, above the frosty twigs, juts a folly like a mandarins hat; it must have been built about the time when *Don Giovanni* was being composed a mile away. Looking-glass regions succeed each other inside the palaces – aqueous reaches under vernal and sunset pastorals where painters and plasterers and cabinet-makers and glaziers and brasiers have fused all their skills in a silence that still seems to vibrate with fugues and passacaglias and the ghosts of commiserating sevenths . . .

Floating downhill, memory scoops new hollows. Churches, echoing marble concavities dim as cisterns in this cloudy weather, celebrate the Counter-Reformation. Plinths round the floor of rotundas hoist stone evangelists aloft. With robes spiraling in ecstasy and mitres like half-open shears, they hover half-way up the twin pillars from whose acanthus-tops the dome-bearing semicircles fly. In one of those churches, where Tridentine fervour had been dulled by two centuries of triumph, there were saints of a less emphatic cast. The figure of St John the Divine – imberb, quizzically smiling, quill in hand and at ease in a dressing-gown with his hair flowing loose like an undress-wig, he might be setting down the first line of *Candide* instead of the Apocalypse; perhaps the sculptor has confused his Enlightenments.

[39] The Chilean Nobel Prize winner for Literature, Pablo Neruda visits his namesake's city in 1960; from *Pablo Neruda: A Passion for Life* by Adam Feinstein, London, 2004.

In October 1920, at the age of sixteen, he [*Ricardo Eliecer Neftalí Reyes Baosoalto*] decided to change his name to Pablo Neruda. It was not an official move – he would not alter his name by deed poll until 28 December 1946 – but from now on, his writings would be signed Pablo Neruda, in an attempt to gain independence, once and for all, from his father's clutches.

The 'Pablo' may have been inspired by Neruda's love of the Italian name Paolo from Italian poetry. His new surname, it is generally believed, was taken from the great Czech writer Jan Neruda [*1834–91*] – Neftalí had read and admired a translation of one of his *Stories from Malá Strana* in a Santiago journal.

. . . [*in 1960*] in Prague, Pablo stopped to admire the houses where his namesake, Jan Neruda, had lived: the House of the Two Suns and the House of the Three Eagles. When [*he*] came to another building, the House of Three Violins, Neruda was entranced. How strange that this instrument should be what enticed Neruda during the visit.

. . . [*when*] the Warsaw Pact troops invaded Czechoslovakia in August 1968, brutally ending the Prague Spring . . . Neruda made no public comment about what was going on in a country he knew well . . . The following year, however, brought Neruda's 1969 collection *Fin de Mundo* (End of the World) . . . In this book we learn something of Neruda's inner response to the news of the Soviet tanks crushing the Prague Spring the year before:

> The hour of Prague fell
>   on my head like a stone,
> my fate was uncertain,
>   a moment of darkness . . .
>   I ask forgiveness for this blind man
>   who saw and didn't see.

The assault on a city where Neruda had shared so many memorable experiences and whose great writer, Jan Neruda, had given him his name, left him genuinely disillusioned and confused.

The Thun Palace

[40] A former British Ambassador to Czechoslovakia (1960–6) tells the colourful story of the embassy building; from *The Serpent and the Nightingale* by Sir Cecil Parrot, London, 1977.

According to Robert Bruce-Lockhart, who spent some dissipated years in it, the British Embassy in Prague, the former Thun-Hohenstein palace, was the most beautiful Ambassadorial residence we had anywhere in the world. It was certainly on the best site, not only by comparison with other embassies, but with all public buildings in Prague, because it bordered on the Hradčany or royal castle – now the President's domain. To the ordinary visitor, who came into the courtyard with its enormous neo-Gothic gateway, it might have appeared a gaunt, if imposing, building, its four storeys crowned by an eighteenth-century pediment and frieze, where the royal coat-of-arms had taken the place of the former Thun-Hohenstein family crest. He could not have suspected that, three flights up, the rooms would open out on to the garden, an enchanting retreat, which enjoyed the most wonderful and certainly the most intimate view both of the castle and the famous Cathedral of St Vitus and which had something of the atmosphere of an English cathedral close.

On the second floor there was a long high terrace where an avenue of trees had once been. Now there is only one very gnarled chestnut, which keeps guard outside the Ambassador's office. This terrace offered a magical view of Prague down to the river Vltava. It used to be the grand climax to a suite of three gorgeous reception rooms. When their chandeliers, some gilt or polychrome wood, and others Venetian or Bohemian glass, were all lit up and reflected in the mirrors on the walls, these three rooms offered a magnificent spectacle. No suite of rooms could have provided a more fitting decor for a really sumptuous ball, where the ladies in grand toilette and regalia would be reflected in the mirrors, and couples could go out on to the terrace in the intervals to enjoy the cooler air. I could see such a scene come to life as I studied one of Count Josef Oswald Thun's invitations from 1836, which the servants of those days had pinned on a door, and was still preserved.

Unhappily, soon after my arrival, the Foreign Office decided to box these rooms up and turn them into offices. The reason was the vulnerability of the Service Attaches who had their offices in the courtyard, the wall of which was exposed to the outside. Someone from outside had managed to make a hole and insert a tube into it, which had presumably been used for photographing or tape-recording. It was this intrusion which persuaded the Foreign Office to move the Service Attaches and some of the outlying departments into the shelter of the main building. I regretted that rooms of unique beauty in the palace and much valuable space for entertaining would be sacrificed just at a time when it was again becoming possible and necessary to make full use of them, but there was no alternative but to submit.

The charm of the Thun Palace lay not only in the beauty and homeliness of the buildings but also in the old butler, Jelínek, who seemed to have become part of them. One Sunday in summer, when we returned early from a drive, we found him in a skull cap, sitting on the stairs and reading the *Guardian*. He chose to sit on the stairs because it was the coolest place on a hot day. The skull cap was to protect his bald head from the draught. Why he read the *Guardian* I cannot exactly say, but he preserved every English newspaper in the house in his room.

I seldom ventured into his sanctuary but managed to have a peep into it now and again. He had several interesting books, mostly antiquarian ones. His window looked down on the garden and the cathedral and he would tempt the squirrels into his room by putting out food for them; the result being that, when he was out of the room, they made hay of it, knocking over his things and scattering food on the floor.

He was a typical Moravian, who could converse with equal fluency in German and Czech. The maids said he was 'noble'. Only our guests could tell how much English he knew. He had served in a great house – at Lancut in Poland for the Potockis, where a footman stood behind every guest at meal times. Later, he worked for Count Doubek, the husband of the famous Czech singer, Jarmila Novotná. He had often been entrusted with his employers' financial dealings. In a Europe torn by faction and dissension it was a blessed relief to find someone so calm, dispassionate and reliable. I once asked him what he thought of the *Good Soldier Švejk*. 'You know, sir,' he said, 'the Austrian officers were not as bad as that. I served under them in the war and some were good people. In any case they were much like the rest of us – good and bad.' Though I knew this of course, it was interesting to hear a Czech confirm it.

Once the decision was taken to rebuild the Embassy we had to face the prospect of a radical transformation of the whole building. This was to be carried out by teams of workmen from England and would take a considerable time, and we ourselves would have to find somewhere else to live. Eventually after much heart searching we reluctantly requisitioned the flat of our hard-worked lady Commercial Secretary and Consul, occupied today by the representative of the British Council.

When we moved back into the renovated residence I made it my business to learn all I could about the beautiful and historic building. Its first recorded owner was alleged to have built it in the fourteenth century, when it 'shone with the splendour of its tower.' During the installation of a lift in 1947, Gothic foundations were revealed, and some of the older Czech workmen found medieval structures round the original Chapel of the Holy Cross on the third floor (converted by the Thun family into a bathroom and used by us as such) and in the winding stairway which led up to the turret. A second circular staircase had originally run from the old first floor to the second, but had been bricked up in more recent times. Under the pool in the garden, repairs revealed the existence of a subterranean chamber or grotto, which also probably went back to medieval times, when the level of the garden may have been lower and the structure situated at ground level.

The palace appears to have been one of the great houses built during the reign of Emperor Charles IV, when the cathedral was rebuilt, the castle restored, the Charles University founded and a new bridge built across the river Vltava. Could any other of our embassies compare with it in antiquity? From its position on the slopes of the Hradčany hill it dominated all that part of Malá Strana which lay between it and the gate tower of the Charles Bridge 300 yards away. From its windows you could see the dreaming spires and roofs of Prague, from the steeple of St Thomas's to the fine patrician house in the square which I imagined belonged to the Montagues until I realized that it was the property of a family called 'Montag'. During the reconstruction in my time some Renaissance frescoes were uncovered representing biblical scenes, possibly Susanna and the Elders. I was glad to be able to preserve them, although they were in our offices.

In 1630 Walter Leslie, a Scottish soldier of fortune and one of the four British mercenaries (two Irishmen, Butler and Deveroux, and two Scotsmen, Gordon and Leslie) who murdered Wallenstein, came into possession of the house. He may have received it in the general 'carve up' after the defeat of the Czech Rising at the Battle of the White Mountain in 1620 or as a gift from a grateful emperor for having helped rid him of a dangerous traitor. At any rate, he achieved great success in Austrian service, numbering among his posts those of Vice-President of the Council of War, Warden of the Sclavonian Marshes, Field-Marshal and Ambassador to the Ottoman Empire, and being decorated with the Order of the Golden Fleece. A memorial to him still stands in the Embassy garden.

He sold the house in 1656 to Count Guidobald Thun-Hohenstein, Archbishop of Salzburg, who, being childless, made a present of it to his brother, Michal Osvald. The latter was an enthusiastic renovator but it was his nephew who had the house rebuilt by the Italian architect, Giovanni Luragho. When we first arrived there was a big room upstairs, which was being used as a ping-pong room, with a four-poster bed in it. This bed was said to have been the Archbishop's and the room was still called the 'Archbishop's Room'. Since the 1960 reconstruction it too has been split up.

Those beautiful reception rooms were boxed up into a horrid labyrinth-registry, archives, bag rooms, etc., and there was nothing left of the dream that had once been. A beautiful spiral staircase leading from the corner of the dining room to the floor above, a speciality of old Prague palaces, was removed so as to create an 'iron curtain' between the Residence and the working part of the Embassy. The Residence was in fact moved a floor higher and reduced from a 'palace' into a 'duplex flat'. Of course, it was more practical for those trying to run it, but now the Foreign Secretary, when he comes to stay, has to sleep in rooms made in the attic alongside the kitchen and the maids' quarters. One Foreign Secretary and his wife complained that the Foreign Office had rebuilt the residence for a race of supermen, as they had to stand on tiptoe to see themselves in the mirrors. On the other hand, the ceilings on the top floor of the *mansarde* were so low that supermen would have bumped their heads on it.

The Wallenstein Palace

___

[41] Albrecht von Wallenstein builds his palatial residence (1623–30); from *Wallenstein* by Francis Watson, London, 1938.

Before he began the acquisition of his estates in the northeast, Wallenstein had planned a noble residence in Prague. The ill-starred Winter King was the last monarch of Bohemia to hold permanent court in the ancient capital that for several generations had been the centre of the Holy Roman Empire. The Austrian Emperor Ferdinand, turning his face from the rebellious city, broke the tradition of his Hapsburg predecessors, and the fulcrum of policy shifted to Vienna. The new aristocracy, enriched with the properties of dispossessed Bohemian nobles, for the most part followed the Emperor, and in Prague Wallenstein was left almost without a rival. A few months after the battle of the White Mountain he bought for demolition a number of the old houses on the hill below the castle, and in 1623 began the building of a palace on the site.

. . . The architects were all Italians. Andrea Spezza prepared the plans, and supervised the construction until his death in 1628, when Nicolo Sebrigondi succeeded him. For the palace was not completed in its original design until four years before Wallenstein's death. The Milanese Guiseppe Marini assisted in the work, and Pironi di Galliano was also consulted. Yet another Italian, Baccio del Bianco, was summoned to decorate the interior, and it may have been he who designed the stucco embellishments of the great hall (*Sala Terrena*) that opens in three lofty arches to the garden. On the ceiling of the audience-chamber, on the first floor, he painted a lively fresco of the charioted Mars, drawn through the clouds by four snorting steeds. The war-god is in seventeenth-century armour, plumed and cloaked.

Above him shines the seven-pointed star of fortune, and his face is the face of Wallenstein. Behind a stately baroque elevation the completed building disposed itself about two courts, the inner one having access to the long garden through the *Sala Terrena*. In the garden wing, at an aloof distance from the sumptuous reception rooms, were the apartments of Wallenstein and his Duchess, not large but finely furnished. A winding stair led from the bathing-grotto on the ground floor to Wallenstein's bedroom, above that to the bedroom of his wife, and above that again to the observatory, since destroyed with all its evidence of science or superstition. There were a small gaming-room, and private oratories for the Duke and Duchess. In Wallenstein's chapel, in an altar-piece of Heidelberg workmanship, the picture that faced him was not that of the Virgin who inspired the dogged career of his master Ferdinand. It represented, symbolically enough, the assassination of his namesake, the Bohemian warrior-king St Wenceslas.

A Dürer and a Cranach, a Carlo Dolci, a contemporary copy of Guido Reni's Head of Christ, and a few more, are all that now remain of Wallenstein's huge and somewhat indiscriminate collection of paintings. In the garden stood a great bronze bowl, surmounted by a statue of Venus, by the Nuremberg Renaissance artist Wurzelbauer, whose fountain of the Virtues still plays beside the *Lorenzkirche* in his native city. It was bought in 1626 from Count Lobkowic to supplement the magnificent collection of garden-bronzes which the Dutchman Adrian de Vries had been carrying out for the Wallenstein Palace. Before the site was well cleared Wallenstein had taken de Vries into his service, and during the next six years no fewer than thirty pieces and groups of statuary were designed and cast. They were carried off by the Swedes after their owner's death, and now adorn the park at Drottningholm, near Stockholm; but the casts made some twenty-five years ago for Wallenstein's descendants suggest the scale on which everything he took in hand was executed.

So, too, does his correspondence with the artist. In February 1626 de Vries writes that he has nearly finished a fountain.

> For the Laocoon with the snakes and two fauns and two sirens and four ducks, four heads of horses and two heads of lions and two heads of griffons, for all this our agreement is 4,500 reichsthaler. If your Highness now prefers to have the Neptune uppermost, that will be ready about Michaelmas and will cost 1,100 reichsthaler, and of the four other pieces now concerned the Apollo will cost 900 reichsthaler, and the group of two wrestlers 1000 reichsthaler and the Bacchus with the child 1,100 reichsthaler, the Adonis and Venus 1,400 reichsthaler, the five pieces together making 5,500 reichsthaler, and 1,000 for the fountain, in all 6,500 reichsthaler.

From the army in Germany, a week after his first great victory, the indefatigable commander forwards to his agent this formidable account:

> What Adrian de Frisa [de Vries] writes to me you shall learn by the enclosed copy. I will take all the pieces. Therefore see that you make an agreement with him on the price, as well as on the date of payment. I desire further that the building shall be carried on steadily this summer, as well in my house as in the mill and court at Prague. Look to it, then, that all is in order, also that my gardens are diligently laid out in accordance with the design. And send the grain to me here immediately.

In two sentences he orders the completion of an elaborate Italian garden and the provision of corn for his army. Both were obeyed by the efficient Gerhard von Taxis, the grain loaded on barges for the long journey down the Elbe, and the grounds at Prague embellished according to detailed plans by an aviary of fantastic grotto-work, in which at one time 400 singing-birds beguiled the fits of war-weariness that periodically attacked their master. At the end of the garden, beyond the pond with the Hercules-statue, a long row of stables housed the finest products of Wallenstein's stud-farms. Their marble drinking-troughs, each fed with running water from a spring, aroused the admiration of Thomas Carve when he visited the palace in 1634.

It was only in the later years of his life, however, that Wallenstein's taste for luxurious state found full expression. As his reputation spread throughout Europe the stages of approach to his person were made commensurately more impressive, and when rulers dealt with him directly it was proper that his own style of living should lack nothing of traditional magnificence. Now and then, in his observatory in Prague, in the council-chamber of a capitulating city or in the busy winter-quarters of his army, he may have dreamed of making his duchy into a kingdom, his kingdom perhaps into an empire. But he built from the ground upwards, and though the Prague palace was from the beginning planned in all its splendour against the time when ambition should be fulfilled, the years of preparation were employed in the conversion of the domain of Friedland to a productive, self-supporting and highly organized territory.

. . . [*in 1627*] his palace was ready for him, as he had ordered; the gardens laid out, the statues of Adrian de Vries a little melancholy in their wintry surroundings, where Neptune and the sirens ruled their basin of ice and only the bronze vine of Bacchus remembered warmth. On the night of his arrival it was the 14th of January – a fire broke out in the palace, and though it was quickly subdued it was regarded in many quarters as an omen. [*Wallenstein was assassinated in Cheb in 1634.*]

The former Rothes Haus
and The Shönborn Palace

[42] On 29 September 1800 Admiral Horatio Nelson celebrates his forty-second birthday in Prague; from *Nelson: A Personal History* by Christopher Hibbert, London, 1994.

Nelson's inn, the former Rothes Haus [*No 8 Karmelitská Street*] was brilliantly illuminated in his honour, a gesture which was less appreciated, so Miss Knight observed, when the cost of the lighting appeared on the bill. The Rothes Haus's distinguished guest created a disappointing impression upon at least one German onlooker, although 'his bold nose, the steady eye and the solid worth revealed in his whole face [*did betray*] in some measure the great conqueror':

> [*Nelson*] was one of the most insignificant figures I ever saw in my life . . . a more miserable collection of bones and wizened frame I have yet to come across . . . He speaks little, and then only English, and he hardly ever smiles. Lady Hamilton behaved like a loving sister towards him; led him, often took

hold of his hand, whispered something into his ear, and he
twisted his mouth into the faintest resemblance of a smile . . .
He was almost covered with orders and stars.

A dinner was held for him at the Archduke's palace where
Lady Hamilton entertained the guests by singing 'God Save
the King', a national anthem which had become popular
in the time of George III's grandfather as a demonstration
of loyalty to him and opposition to the Jacobites. Lady
Hamilton also sang some verses written by Miss Knight, who
was always more than ready to oblige with lines on such
occasions and who, according to an unfriendly observer,
never opened her mouth except to flatter her friends. At the
end of September the Admiral's party left Prague for Dresden.

[43] A young American diplomat at the United States
Legation in Prague, the former Shönborn Palace, is
asked to escort a future US president on his brief visit
to the capital in 1938; from *Memoirs: 1925 – 1950* by
George F. Kennan, Boston, 1967.

In those days [*October 1938*], as the German forces
advanced like encroaching waves over all the borders in
Bohemia, no trains were running, no planes were flying, no
frontier stations existed. Yet in the midst of this confusion
we [*the United States legation staff*] received a telegram
from the embassy in London, the sense of which was that
our ambassador there, Mr Joseph Kennedy, had chosen this
time to send one of his young sons on a fact-finding tour
around Europe, and it was up to us to find means of getting
him across the border and through the German lines so that
he could include in his itinerary a visit to Prague.

We were furious. Joe Kennedy was not exactly known as
a friend of the career service, and many of us, from what we
had heard about him, cordially reciprocated this lack of
enthusiasm. His son [*John F.*] had no official status and was,
in our eyes, obviously an upstart and ignoramus. The idea
that there was anything he could learn or report about conditions in Europe which we did not already know and had

not already reported seemed (and not without reason) wholly absurd. That busy people should have their time taken up arranging his tour struck us as outrageous. With that polite but weary punctiliousness that characterizes diplomatic officials required to busy themselves with pesky compatriots who insist on visiting places where they have no business to be, I arranged to get him through the German lines, had him escorted to Prague, saw to it that he was shown what he wanted to see, expedited his departure, then, with a feeling of 'that's that,' washed my hands of him – as I thought. Had anyone said to me then that the young man in question would some day be the President of the United States and that I, in the capacity of chief of diplomatic mission, would be his humble and admiring servant, I would have thought that either my informant or I have taken leave of my senses.

THE CHARLES BRIDGE AND THE VLTAVA

[44] The martyrdom of St Jan Nepomuk in 1393; from *A Time of Gifts* by Patrick Leigh Fermor, London, 1977.

It took me a little time to realize that the Vltava and the Moldau were the Czech and the German names for the same river. It flows through the capital as majestically as the Tiber and the Seine through their offspring cities; like them, it is adorned with midstream islands and crossed by noble bridges. Among crowding churches and a mist of trees, two armoured barbicans prick their steeples like gauntlets grasping either end of a blade and between them flies one of the great medieval bridges of Europe. Built by Charles IV, it is a rival to Avignon and Regensburg and Cahors and a stone epitome of the city's past. Sixteen tunnelling spans carry it over the flood. Each arc springs from a massive pier and the supporting cutwaters advance into the rush of the current like a line of forts. High overhead and every few yards along either balustrade stand saints or groups of saints and as one gazes along the curve of the bridge, the teams unite in a flying population; a backward glance through one of the barbicans reveals the facade of a church where yet another holy flock starts up from a score of ledges. At the middle of one side and higher than the rest, stands St Johannes [*Jan*] Nepomuk. He was martyred a few yards away in 1393 – he is said to have refused, under torture, to betray a confessional secret of Queen Sophia. When the henchmen of Wenceslas IV carried him here and hurled him into the Vltava, his drowned body, which was later retrieved and entombed in the Cathedral, floated downstream under a ring of stars.

[45] 'All life in Prague centres round the Charles Bridge' observes an Englishman in his late nineteenth-century travel guide; from *Pictures from Bohemia* by James Baker, London, 1897.

All life in Prague centres round the Carls [*Charles*] Bridge, just as in Athens the traveller hastens on his arrival to climb the Acropolis, and returns again and again to look out from amidst its temples over modern Athens, so in Prague the Carls Bridge draws all visitors to its statuted arches, there to look around at the city, with its towers, and pinnacles, and clustered buildings, stretching away on either side of the swift rushing Moldau [*Vltava*]. But although the Carls Bridge cannot claim the antiquity of the Acropolis, yet it not only represents a great dead past, but it still is the centre of all the busy life in Prague of to-day.

[46] 'The Bridge' – a poem by Franz Kafka, from *Kafka and Prague* by Johann Bauer, translated by P. S. Falla, London, 1971.

> Men and women crossing dark bridges,
> Past the statues of saints
> with their faint glimmer of light.
> Clouds drifting over gray skies,
> Past churches
> With misty towers.
> A man leaning over the parapet
> And gazing into the river at evening,
> His hands resting on ancient stone.

[47] The old stone bridge is the physical and spiritual centre of Prague and represents the, 'peculiar invulnerability of the city'; from *The Spirit of Prague* by Ivan Klíma, London, 1994.

For me, the material and spiritual centre of the city is an almost 700-year-old stone bridge connecting the west with the east. The Charles Bridge is an emblem of the city's situation in Europe, the two halves of which have been seeking each other out at the very least since the bridge's foundations were laid. The West and the East. Two branches of the same culture, yet representing two differing traditions, different tribes of the peoples of Europe.

It also represents the peculiar invulnerability of this city, its capacity to recover from disasters. For centuries, it has withstood the high waters that regularly flood Prague. Only once, two centuries ago, has it suffered, when two of its arches collapsed, taking pedestrians with them into the swollen waters. But the bridge was quickly repaired, and today the citizens of Prague no longer know anything about an event that contemporary chroniclers considered one of the worst catastrophes ever to afflict the city.

[*The 2001 floods made the citizens of Prague painfully aware that, to this day, the Vltava can cause a disaster on an unprecedented scale. ed.*]

THE OLD TOWN

The Clementinum

---

[48] From their barricades in the Old Town the Czechs fight the Imperial Austrian army during the bloody 1848 rising; from *The Czech Revolution of 1848* by Stanley Z. Pech, North Carolina, 1969.

The Uprising lasted six days, from Monday, June 12, until Saturday, June 17. The rebels had the advantage of controlling the short, narrow streets running in various directions in the heart of the city on the east bank of the river Moldau [*Vltava*], for these streets could easily be barricaded and held even against the superior might of the army. The headquarters of the rebels was the Clementinum, a complex of university buildings in the Old Town of Prague. Shortly after the outbreak of the uprising, Governor Thun hurried to the Old Town to plead personally with the students to desist from violence. The sight of the governor climbing the barricades, impeccably clad and wearing a top hat, was a rare one indeed. The impressive countenance and attire did not prevent Thun from being seized as a hostage later in the day, to be used by the rebels as a lever against

General Windischgrätz. But Governor Thun absolutely refused to be a party to any mediation or negotiation in such circumstances; he showed himself throughout as entirely fearless, and his courageous conduct earned him the esteem of friend and foe alike. On Tuesday the rebels released him after some of the Czech leaders interceded on his behalf.

Windischgrätz acquired something of a personal stake in the crushing of the rebels as a result of a tragedy that struck as close as a tragedy could: his wife was killed by a stray bullet on the first day of the fighting.

. . . The uprising was a spontaneous outbreak deeply rooted in the mood of the city. And if one were to reduce the emotions of the citizens of Prague to a single common denominator, that denominator would have been a thorough dislike of General Windischgrätz. No man had been more hated in recent memory. He was abhorred by radicals and moderates alike, by men and women, and by young and old.

. . . He finally bombarded the city into submission, compelling it to capitulate on June 17. On the next day a state of siege was declared in Prague and the adjacent area, and a roundup of revolutionary suspects began.

. . . The guiding and driving force of the June Uprising was the university students, and among these, the majority were probably from the Polytechnic, despite the fact that they represented a minority of the total student population in Prague.

The most striking characteristic of the barricade-fighters of whatever social class was their youth. The students were all young, and their youth was matched, in the ranks of the workers, by journey men, apprentices, and young workers generally. This was also the pattern in uprisings in other cities in Europe.

Among the young were not only men but also women. Even a group of students in a girls' school lent an eager hand in the building of the barricades; their teachers were fainting from fright but the intrepid maidens opened the windows of the school and enthusiastically hurled benches and tables out into the street. The Czech politician and poet Josef Václav Frič , ever alert to the romantic and the erotic, said that 'the fair sex showed itself particularly sympathetic to us. Ladies, attired for a promenade and holding parasols, gazed at the persevering defenders of the barricades, flirted here and there with the younger ones, hopped over the barricades like chamois . . .' Girls cared for the wounded and some even carried arms. The sight of young women on the barricades was not easily forgotten, and the courage of these heroines was celebrated in a contemporary popular song. The uprising also produced its 'Amazon,' whom observers remembered as a girl with short, loose hair, clad in a Slavic costume, sitting on the main barricade and holding a musket in her hand.

The Theatre on the Balustrade

[49] The former Czech President, Václav Havel, recalls his theatrical beginnings in the late 1950s; from *Disturbing the Peace*, New York, 1990.

It was with [*the play* If a Thousand Clarinets] that the Theatre on the Balustrade began. There were no professional actors in it. I saw a performance during one of my army leaves; I can't recall whether I liked it or not, but I remember being fascinated by the atmosphere of the theatre. It looked different then. In one corner of the hall there was an enormous old coal-burning stove; the first generation of those little lamps we called *kondeliky* were flickering on the walls. Many of the audience stood on the balcony outside the building and watched performances through the windows (later, when my wife was an usher, she had endless problems with this phenomenon). It was all somewhat reminiscent of a nightclub. (By the way – and I don't know exactly why this is, and someday I'm going to have to give some thought to it – an inseparable part of the kind of theatre I've been drawn to all my life is a touch of obscurity, of decay or degeneration, of frivolity, I don't know quite what to call it; I think theatre should always be somewhat suspect.) No matter how the performance turned out, one thing was certain: it was full of the joy of performance, there was freedom, pure humour, and intelligence in it; it didn't take itself too seriously, and people were delighted. In short, something new and unprecedented was born.

. . . That period was extremely important for me, not only because those eight years in the Theatre on the Balustrade were in fact the only period when I was able to devote myself fully to theatre, to the only kind of theatre that interested me, but also because it formed me as a playwright. I gave myself over to my work with an almost preposterous enthusiasm; I was in the theatre from morning to evening, and at night, with my wife's help, we made the scenery. It was like a joyous intoxication. After a time, I settled down and became more down-to-earth about it, but up until 1968, when I left, I lived for that theatre, I helped to create its profile, and I identified with it entirely. I went through a number of jobs when I was there, from stagehand to lighting technician, secretary, reader, right up to dramaturge. But it didn't really matter which of those jobs I held in any given moment, and often I held them concurrently: in the morning I organized tours, in the evening I ran the lighting for the performance, and at night I rewrote plays.

[50] In the mid-1960s, one of London's foremost theatre producers meets three of Prague's most successful experimental theatre artists; from *My World of Theatre* by Peter Daubeny, London, 1971.

By and large the Czech arts have always been linked with everyday life – particularly from the early nineteenth century, when they first came to be used as an ideological and political weapon in the struggle for national emancipation. Theatre has always formed an integral part of the general cultural scene. More than that: it used to be – and to some extent still is – almost a place of worship. It is significant that in popular parlance the Czech National Theatre is called 'our chapel'. When its superb house was burnt down in 1881 it was a national tragedy. People wept in the streets, and it was rebuilt within only two years from private donations in which the whole nation participated. The nation's gift to itself is its motto, engraved in large gold letters above the stage. It has been a place of pilgrimage for country people from near and far, a symbol of the Czech cultural heritage and of national unity.

The Theatre on the Balustrade followed in the wake of the release from the Stalinist period of 'desiccated, didactic and dehumanized art'. It was founded in 1958 by Vladimír Vodička, its administrator, and Ladislav Fialka, the brilliant mime, who had already been leading his own troupe since 1953. In 1959 the triumvirate was completed by Jan Grossman, who became artistic director of the drama group.

One evening, after seeing Fialka's troupe at the theatre in the beautiful old quarter of Prague, I dined with these three directors in one of the tiny cellar restaurants near the theatre. We talked first of Fialka and his mime group, whom I had just seen in *The Fools*. Unlike most modern mimes, Fialka does not work alone, but as the leader of a closely knit, compact group. It was obvious from watching the dreamlike qualities of *The Fools* that it was the result of an evolution which the group had worked out for themselves among themselves.

'We felt sometimes as though we were doing something which had no logical sense,' he told me. 'But we knew that this was the key to the sense of everything. We felt like fools, and I gave this title to the performance.' Fialka's mimes are exquisite blends of pantomime, dance and drama. 'But for us,' added Grossman, 'the most important thing is the audience. We aim at creating a kind of dialogue between actor and audience, so that both can be personally involved in what goes on stage.'

In their little studio theatre it is undoubtedly easier to attain this relationship than in the large auditorium of the Aldwych, but his superb production of Jarry's *King Ubu*, which came as part of the 1968 season, illustrated perfectly the aspects of the Theatre on the Balustrade which have made it such an exciting and respected theatre throughout Europe. The impeccable timing was a tribute to the long hours of discussion and rehearsal which precede every production.

For their first appearance in London in 1967 Grossman's drama group had brought a dramatization of Kafka's novel *The Trial*, the story of Josef K, who 'without having done anything wrong was arrested one fine morning.' Grossman attempted to do more than merely present Kafka's story on the stage; he had tried to capture an aspect of Prague which had always fascinated me. This was the Prague which had existed as an entity in Kafka's mind during his years of spiritual exile in Berlin; the Prague of a man at the mercy of his own fears, and cut off from the world by a destructive process of self-examination and the agony of his sense of guilt.

The Bethlehem Chapel

[51] A young priest, Jan Hus, much influenced by the teachings of John Wycliffe, preached here from 1402 to 1413; from *Essays in Czech History* by R. R. Betts, London, 1969.

Jan Hus's radical sermons and outspokeness against some practices of the Catholic Church prompted his unofficial trial at the Council of Constance in 1415. He refused to renounce his beliefs and was burned at stake as a heretic, becoming overnight a Czech national hero. The following well-known passage was written by Hus in 1412:

Lo, I rely on this most holy and fruitful example of the Redeemer and, from the heavy oppression, wrongful sentence, and pretended excommunication of the pontiffs, scribes, pharisees and judges sitting in Moses' seat I appeal to God, committing my cause to Him. I follow in the footsteps of my Saviour Jesus Christ as did the great and holy patriarch of Constantinople, John Chrysostom, from the crafty Council of bishops and clerics; as Andrew, blessed in hope, bishop of Prague and Robert of Lincoln, when they were harmfully oppressed, humbly and healthfully appealed from the Pope to the supreme and most just Judge, who is never moved by fear, nor turned aside by love, nor seduced by gifts, nor deceived by false witnesses.

I hope therefore that all the faithful of Christ, and especially the princes, barons, knights, vassals and other inhabitants of the kingdom of Bohemia will understand and sympathize with me in this pretended excommunication which I suffer mainly through the instigation of my rival and adversary Michael de Causis, formerly incumbent of the church of St Adalbert in the New Town of Prague; an excommunication which was given and fulminated by Peter of S. Angelo, cardinal deacon of the Roman Church, as the judge deputed by the Roman pontiff John XXII, who for two years refused to give audience to my advocates and proctors, which should not be denied even to Jew, pagan or heretic; nor was he willing to accept any reasonable excuse that I did not appear in person, nor to accept in his fatherly kindness the evidence of the university of the Studium of Prague, even with the seal and attestation of notaries public called in evidence . . .

I, Jan Hus of Husinec, master of arts, bachelor formatus of sacred theology of the university of Prague, priest and preacher appointed to the Chapel called Bethlehem, make hereby my appeal to the Lord Jesus Christ, the most just judge who knows, protects and judges, makes plain and unfailingly rewards the just cause of every man.

The Old Town Square and the Old Town Hall

[52] The tragic story of Master Hanuš of Růže who built the Astronomical Clock (Orloj) in the 1390s; from *The Old Czech Legends* by Alois Jirásek translated by Edith Pargeter, Prague, 1963.

Hordes of people flocked to the City Hall in the Old Town, and yet there was neither a town meeting being held, nor an important trial, but still they kept coming. They all stood around waiting expectantly, for an hour or more, in crowded discomfort. They were there to gaze at the tower with its wonder of wonders, the new clock. Everybody was talking about it – in all the quarters of the city, inside noble palaces, in poor people's houses, in taverns and shops, and on the streets: this new clock in the City Hall tower in the Old Town was not like other clocks, but was so marvellous that there was no other like it in the whole world. [. . .] They spoke of the clock's originator, endowed with special gifts and talents; all admired Master Hanuš, who had built it.

Even learned men from the university, masters and doctors in their academic robes, standing together as they examined the clock, had praise for its builder. They spoke in Latin, solemnly, with grave faces. But they discussed only the circles and lines and signs on the dial.

The learned masters grew silent as a group of councilmen and Old Town officials, all in ceremonial garb, made their way through the ornate portal, heading for the clock tower. The crowd parted to make way for them, and all eyes turned on them, especially on one pale-faced, dark-haired elderly man. He was clad in the dark robes of a master of his craft, and walked right next to the governor. The word got around that this was Master Hanuš, the maker of the clock. People crowded around, craning their necks to get a glimpse of him.

Everybody, even the people from the university, greeted him respectfully. He responded with courtesy, and as soon as the city fathers stopped under the clock, he at once proceeded to explain its workings. One of the professors of Charles University who had come along told the assembled company that he had travelled far and wide, and had visited Italy and France, where he had seen some fine big clocks, but never had he seen the like of this one. 'I do not believe that a more magnificent one could be found anywhere else in the whole world,' he said, 'unless Master Hanuš himself should build it.'

The governor gave a start and glanced at his councillors, who quickly returned his look. All had simultaneously been struck by the same thought: that such a thing might happen. They turned to Hanuš, who smiled, and said disarmingly that he was happy to have been able to complete this complex clock, and that he thanked God for having done so. But the governor left the clock tower less happily than he had entered it. A worrisome thought had been planted in his mind, as well as in the minds of the elders: namely, that Master Hanuš might make another such clock elsewhere, that other places would then have such a marvel of their own.

The fame of the Prague clock spread over the crown lands of Bohemia and into foreign countries. Every visitor who came to town went to see it, and then talked about it after he returned home. Messengers came from various towns, at home and abroad, to ask Master Hanuš to build a similar clock for them. The governor and his council grew uneasy. They did not wish to share their glory with anyone; they wanted their clock to remain the only one of its kind. They sat in secret session to consider what should be done to this end. They agreed that Hanuš might be tempted by foreign promises of a reward. Perhaps he was already at work on a new clock, they thought, a clock that would be even better, since he spent so much time in his workshop, working on something or other. In order to make sure that nobody would compete with them, they decided to commit a terrible deed.

Master Hanuš was seated in his workshop behind a large table, and was busy drawing plans for some complex machinery on a large sheet of paper, by the light of two candles. The shutters were drawn, and there was a fire burning in the fireplace. It was night. The street outside was dark and deserted. The house, too, was quiet. The clock maker was so absorbed in his task that he did not hear footsteps on the stairs outside. He did not even turn around when the door opened and three men came in, wearing cloaks and hoods that covered much of their faces. Only after they had come up to him did he stop his work to look at them. But before he had time to ask what they wanted, two of them seized him while the third blew out the candles. Then they gagged him and pulled him to the glowing fireplace.

These men had let themselves in with a pass key, and nobody in the household knew of their presence or heard their muffled footsteps, either as they entered or as they left the house. They had come like shadows, and like shadows they disappeared into the night. It was not until the following morning that their crime was discovered. The apprentices found Master Hanuš, still gagged, racked with fever, and with a bandage over his eyes. Then Hanuš told his horrified household and neighbours what had happened. The intruders had put his eyes out and placed the bandage around his head. He could not remember much more, as he had passed out.

This, he felt, was his reward. He fretted more and more and his body grew weaker and weaker. Finally, he felt that his end was near. Mustering his last bit of strength, he had one of his former apprentices lead him to the city hall in the Old Town. As usual, a crowd had gathered by the tower, waiting for the clock to strike. But nobody recognized him, he had aged so much. He was thinner, his cheeks sunken, his hair grey, his skin the colour of parchment. At the door he met several of the councillors, but they avoided him. Nobody greeted him. None of them had been pleased when he had sent word he was coming, that he had had a new idea about how to improve the clock so the weights would move more smoothly.

He had his guide take him to the fourth part of the clock-works, the most complex of all. In his darkness he could only hear the clicking and ticking of the many parts. As he stood there, listening, he thought of the council, of how blindness had been his reward, of how the council had made him suffer, only to be able to boast before the whole world of his great achievement.

Just then, the bell started to toll, the figure of Death outside pulling the rope. The fleeting hour was announced. Death called. The windows opened, the apostles started revolving. Master Hanuš trembled. He held out his right hand over the clockwork, and then, as though he could see clearly, his bony fingers began manipulating the machinery. When he drew back his hand, the wheels started revolving madly, ticking and squeaking, roaring and ticking. Then they ground to a standstill. The figures froze where they stood. The apostles did not complete their hourly journey. The cock did not crow. Outside, the excited throng screamed. The councilmen ran to the tower. But the clockworks stood motionless, and their builder lay on the floor beside them in a dead faint. He was carried home and died soon afterward.

The clock continued to stand still, as there was no one to repair it. Only much later was it somewhat restored and is working to this day, a matchless curiosity.

[53] The public execution in the Old Town Square on 21 June 1621 of twenty-seven Protestant leaders who were condemned to death following the battle of the White

Mountain fought the previous year; from *History of the Church* by Pavel Skála of Zhoře.

The imperial executioners appeared before the lords, saying that the hour of death had come, that they should be ready, and that each one whose name was called should come out (of the prison). Immediately afterwards the judges entered the prison and called out the name of Count Schlick. With them arrived four German priests, and when they had descended the steps, two Jesuits stood there, one of whom was called Sudetius.

After him they called out the name of Venceslas of Budova. He took no clergyman with him.

Meanwhile Harant of Polžic sent for John the clergyman, asking him to come, as it would soon be his turn.

. . . Then Lord Harant said, sighing, 'O my dear God, through how many lands have I travelled, how many dangers have I encountered, for how many days have I not seen bread; once I have been buried in the sands. From all these perils God has rescued me, and now I must die guiltless in my own dear land. Forgive my enemies, O my dear Lord.' Then they called out his name, and he started for that mournful stage and slaughterhouse of Antichrist.

But this is worthy of notice, that when one of these holy men and martyrs for God's cause was called forth, then to our great astonishment a leave-taking occurred in a pleasant manner, which rejoiced our hearts, just as if they were preparing to go to a banquet or some pastime. 'Now, my dear friends, may our Lord God bless you, may He grant you the consolations of the Holy Ghost, patience and courage, so that you may be able to prove, now also in the moment of your death, that you have heartily and bravely defended the honour of God. I go before you that I may first see the glory of God, the glory of our beloved Redeemer, but I await you directly after me; already in this hour earthly grief vanishes, and a new heart-felt and eternal gladness begins.'

The other prisoners who remained behind answered, 'May our Lord God bless you on your way for the sake of the guiltless death of Christ; may he send His holy angels to meet your soul. You go before us to the glory of heaven. We also will follow you, and we are certain because of Him in whom we have believed, Jesus Christ, that we shall all meet again to-day and rejoice for ever with our beloved Redeemer, the angels, and the chosen of God.' . . . But let us return to the account of the last journey and the words of the dying. When leaving the prison-room Harant said, 'In thee, my God, I have believed since my youth; do not let me be disgraced for all ages.' Meanwhile, John the clergyman was saying prayers till they reached the place of execution, then Harant said, lifting his eyes heavenwards, 'Into your hands, Lord Jesus Christ, I commend my soul.' And then he was beheaded, and exchanged this wretched earthly light for a glorious and heavenly one.

And the executioner, who was himself a Utraquist, was careful not to interrupt their prayer; and he always waited till each of them had finished his devotions.

[54] The Prague executioner Jan Mydlář and his macabre role in 'one of the bitterest tragedies in Bohemian history' played out outside the Old Town Hall on 21 June 1621; from *Magic Prague* by Angello Maria Ripellino, translated by David Newton Marinelli, London, 1994.

On 18 June 1621 the Prague executioner Jan Mydlář received an order to erect a scaffold for the execution of twenty-seven Czech dignitaries (nobles, knights and burghers) condemned to death for having led a revolt against the Habsburgs. That very night, working by torchlight in the Old Town Square, the executioner's assistants began construction of a *theatrum* four ells high and twenty-two paces long and wide. It was enclosed by a wooden railing, linked by a narrow bridge to a balcony of the Old Town Hall (which served as a backdrop) and covered to the ground with black cloth.

At five o'clock on 21 June, a day of infamy in Bohemian history, the Castle cannons gave the signal for the ignominious spectacle to begin. The *theatrum* emerged as the tentative light of dawn relieved the darkness. Two detachments of light cavalry and three infantry companies had been summoned to keep the throng at bay. One of Mydlář's assistants, his head draped in black, set up a crucifix in front of the block, next to which Mydlář himself waited with bared sword and a face as hard as cold quince. The coffins stood ready beneath the scaffolding as in a crypt. Haughty magistrates clad in black sat on the Town Hall balcony, three of them walking back and forth from the scaffold to summon the condemned one by one.

The drums rolled and the trumpets blared throughout the execution to prevent the mob from hearing the groans and last words of the executed men, whose heads continued to twitch on the sand-covered floorboards after being separated from their torsos. Six servants of the executioner, the *holomci*, wearing black masks and black cloaks, carried off the truncated cadavers so the executioner might avoid touching any of the wretches he had dispatched with his sword. 'An atrocious spectacle,' the poet Dačický writes: black scaffold, black dress, black masks. The square, as [*the Czech writer*] Machar later claimed in a poem, was a true Golgotha.

The executions went on for four hours, the infallible executioner using four swords to decapitate twenty-four notables. As a kind of interlude, a respite from his labours, he hanged the other three: one from a gallows erected in the centre of the square and two from a beam jutting out of a Town Hall window. In the aforementioned poem by Machar, the hangman, worn-out and thirsty, recounts the details to his wife, cynically boasting – while waiting for a servant girl to bring him a mug of beer at the Green Frog inn – of having severed each head with a single blow.

. . . Mydlář not only swung the sword and tightened the nooses but embellished upon the proceedings by chopping off the right hand of Ondřej Šlik, Bohuslav of Michalovice, Jiřík Hauenšild and Leander Ripl, and hacking out the tongue of the rector of Prague University, Johannes Jessenius, before delivering the *coups de grace*. Jessenius' headless corpse was moved to the field outside the Horská brána – the gate to the road for Kutná Hora – where it was quartered and impaled on posts.

Shortly before noon Mydlář returned to the ill-fated *theatrum* to collect twelve heads, which he carried in iron baskets to the Stone Bridge to expose them to ridicule on the cornice of the Bridge Tower – six facing Malá Strana, six facing the Catholic Church of the Holy Saviour. He nailed the severed right hands of Count Šlik and Dr Hauenšild to their heads and Jessenius' tongue to his.

Except for the skull of Count Šlik, which was returned to his family in May 1622, the heads remained suspended in their iron baskets for a decade. Not until a band of Czech émigrés entered Prague with the Protestant Saxons in 1631 were they removed from the Tower and interred in Týn Church with due ceremony. Yet even though in 1766 a coffin containing eleven skulls was exhumed in the church, popular wisdom has it that the heads were buried in a secret place in the Protestant Church of the Holy Saviour and that every year on the anniversary of the execution they rise and visit Old Town Square to make certain the hands of Master Hanuš's astrological clock have not stopped: when they stop, doom is nigh.

Thus on 21 June 1621 one of the bitterest tragedies in Bohemian history was played out. The executioner Jan Mydlář, instrument of the vengeance and treacherous bigotry of Ferdinand II, secured the rout and subjugation of a people of rebels and heretics with his unerring swords.

[55] In 1841 Hans Christian Andersen visits the tombstone of the Danish astronomer Tycho Brahe inside the Church of Our Lady of Týn (located on the fifth pillar on the right); from *Poet's Bazaar* translated by Charles Beckwith, London, 1846.

(Tycho Brahe, 1546–1601, a Danish astronomer and mathematician, was the most accomplished and systematic observer of the skies before the use of telescopes. In 1576 Frederick II gave Brahe the island of Hven, where he built the observatory of Uraniborg ['Castle of the Heavens']. In 1597 he was forced to leave Denmark and in 1599 Brahe arrived in Prague at the behest of Rudolf II.)

Aloft on the mountain, with prospect over city, river, and wood-grown isles, lies old Hradschin. The church here contains the body of St Nepomuk in a magnificent silver coffin. What pomp within, what splendid scenery without! And yet this is not the place that the Dane visits first in Prague. Down by the market-place is a poor little church; – a piazza and a narrow yard lead to it. The priest says mass before the altar; the congregation kneel, and mumble an '*Ora pro nobis!*' It sounds like a hollow, mournful sigh from the abyss; it pours forth like a painful sob, a cry of lamentation. The Dane wanders through the isle to the right; a large red-brown stone, in which is carved a knight in armour, is walled in the pillar. Whose bones lie mouldering within? A countryman's! a Dane's! a master-spirit! whose name sheds a lustre over Denmark – that land which expelled him. His castle at home is sunken in rubbish; the plough-share passes over the spot where he, in his cheerful room, searched the writings, and received the visits of Kings; the sea-gull flies through the air, where he read the stars from his tower; – his island of life and happiness in strange hands. Denmark does not own it; Denmark owns not even his dust; but the Danes mention his name in their bad times, as if a denunciation proceeded out of it: 'These are Tycho Brahe's days!' say they.

The Dane weeps by Tycho's grave in a foreign land, and becomes wrathful against an undiscerning age. [. . .] A sunbeam falls on the grave-stone – perhaps a tear also! The congregation mumble their evaporating, painful, '*Ora pro nobis!*'

[56] In 1919 Franz Kafka reproaches his father, Herman, for mistreating the employees at his shop situated on the ground floor of the Kinský Palace; from *Letter to my father* (unsent).

I could enjoy what you gave, but only in humiliation, weariness, weakness, and with a sense of guilt. That was why I could be grateful to you for everything only as a beggar is, and never show it by doing the right things.

The next external result of this whole method of upbring-
ing was that I fled from everything that even remotely
reminded me of you. First there was the business. In itself,
particularly in my childhood, so long as it was a shop,
I ought to have liked it very much, it was so animated, the
lights lit at evening, so much to see and hear, being able to
help now and then and to distinguish oneself, but above all
to admire you for your magnificent commercial talents, the
way you sold things, managed people, made jokes, were
untiring, knew the right decision to make at once in doubt-
ful cases, and so forth; even the way you wrapped up a
parcel or opened a crate was a spectacle worth watching,
and all this was certainly not the worst school for a child.
But since you gradually began to terrify me on all sides and
the business and you became one for me, the business too
made me feel uneasy. Things that had at first been a matter
of course for me there now began to torment and shame me,
particularly the way you treated the staff.

I don't know, perhaps it was like that in most business, . . .
but in my childhood other businesses did not concern me.
But you I heard and saw shouting, cursing, and raging in the
shop, in a way that in my opinion at that time had not its
equal anywhere in the world. And not only cursing, but other
sorts of tyrannizing. For instance, the way you would push
goods you did not want to have mixed up with others, knocking them off the counter – only the thoughtlessness of your
rage was some slight excuse – and the assistant had to pick
them up. Or your constant mode of referring to an assistant
with T. B. lungs: 'Sooner he dies the better, the mangey dog.'
You called the employees 'paid enemies', and that was what
they were too, but even before they became such you seemed
to me to be their 'paying enemy'. There too I learnt the great
lesson that you could be unjust; in my own case I would not
have noticed it so soon, for here was too much accumulated
sense of guilt, ready to admit that you were right; but there,
in my childish view, later of course a little but not overmuch
corrected, were strangers, who were after all working for us
and because of that had to live in constant dread of you.

JOSEFOV

The old Prague Ghetto

[57] A famous sixteenth-century legend retold by a twentieth-century author; from *The Golem* by Eduard Petiška, Prague, 1994.

When the waves of hatred against the Jews rose again, Rabbi Loew was expected to help rescue them. They told him:

'Each night somebody can bring secretly a dead man to the ghetto and accuse us of murder. You can still find many people who believe the stories that we need Christian blood for our rituals.'

High Rabbi Loew listened to the representatives of the community and nodded seriously:

'I am worried just like you,' he said, 'but don't be afraid, I promise to help you soon.'

The elders of the Jewish community left, and Rabbi Loew prayed long into the night, so as to be inspired with a dream and with good advice.

He went to bed late, and when he closed his eyes, a dream came to him. In the dream he saw an inscription running: *Make a golem of clay – a figure similar to man. The golem will help you against your enemies.*

The following morning, as soon as the rabbi woke up, he had his son-in-law and one of his pupils called immediately.

'I have called you,' he told them, 'because I received a command from Heaven in the night to make a creature of clay resembling man, a golem. We need four elements for this task: Earth, Water, Fire, and Air. I feel in myself the power of Air, you, my son-in-law, will represent the power of Fire, and you, my dear pupil, will represent Water. The fourth element, Earth, we shall find in a place favourable to our purpose. We shall part now. For seven days we shall be concentrating and preparing our minds in order to succeed in this matter.'

For seven days Rabbi Loew, his son-in-law, and his pupil prepared for the unusual task. On the seventh day each of them bathed in the *mikvah*, the ritual Jewish bath, in accordance with the custom of their ancestors. Then they dressed in white clothes, and with a prayer on their lips, set out on their journey outside the city.

The clock struck four, when the darkness is thickest, and brings to mind the moment before the creation of the world. Outside the city they found a spot on the bank of the Vltava, where there was enough intact wet earth, carried from the mountains by the river. They lit their torches and continued praying and reciting the Psalms.

They made a shape of a man, three ells tall, from mould-able clay. Then they put it on the ground, and by gentle movements of their fingers marked out its mouth, nose, eyes and ears, giving human features to its face. Then they imitated human legs, arms, hands and fingers. Finally the figure of the golem lay in front of them. It resembled a man lying on his back.

'You represent the element of Fire,' said Rabbi Loew to his son-in-law, 'walk round the golem seven times, while saying the lines I have written for you.'

The rabbi's son-in-law walked round the golem, while saying the lines in a clear voice. When he made the first round, the golem became dry. When be made the third round, the golem glowed with heat. And when he was finishing the seventh round, the golem glowed and gleamed white-hot like iron in a smith's furnace.

Then the rabbi ordered his pupil who represented the element of Water to walk round the golem seven times too, saying his lines.

The pupil obeyed. During the first round the red gleam of the golem's trunk died out. When he made the third round, little clouds of vapour issued from the golem's surface and his body grew damp. During the following rounds, nails grew on his fingers, his head became covered with hair and his skin acquired a faint human lustre.

In his stature and appearance he resembled a man of thirty.

Then Rabbi Loew himself repeated the same procedure. During the seventh round, he opened the golem's mouth and inserted the *shem*, a parchment inscribed with God's name. Finally the rabbi, his son-in-law and his pupil bowed to all the cardinal points, while pronouncing together the following sentence: 'Lord made a man from the clay of the Earth and breathed the breath of life into his mouth.'

After these words, life arose in the clay from which the golem had been made. Fire, Water and Air awoke him. He exhaled, and looked in amazement at those who had called him to life.

'Rise,' Rabbi Loew ordered him.

And the golem rose, just as people rise after a long sleep. He straightened up and stood before his makers.

Now all that remained was to dress him. They had brought with them the clothes that were worn by the servants of the synagogue. They dressed him in these clothes, just as a person is dressed. They also showed him how to put on his shoes, and he did so. Now he looked like other people. He lacked only one thing – human speech. He was mute. Heaven kept the secret of giving the gift of speech to itself and did not share it with High Rabbi Loew. To perform the tasks for which the golem had been made, he did not have to talk. He was only to hear and obey.

The day was dawning and the red morning sky coloured the surface of the Vltava and the clay bed from which the golem had risen. It was time to return.

On the way back the rabbi said to him:

'We made you from clay and gave you life, in order to protect the Jews against their enemies and against persecution. I give you the name Joseph. You will live in my house and obey my orders. You'll do everything I order you even if I order you to throw yourself out of a tower, even if I send you to the depths of the sea.' Joseph nodded in agreement. He could hear and understand, but could not command his tongue.

[58] The seventeenth-century French physician Charles Patin visits the Prague Ghetto in the second half of the seventeenth century; from *Travels thro' Germany, Bohemia, Swisserland, Holland and other Parts of Europe*, London, 1697.

At Prague [*the Jews*] haue the priuileges of Cittizens, but they buye it and continue it with great payments of money, as well imposed on them by the Pope, as by free guift of large sommes to the Emperour, and firnishing him with money upon occasions.

. . . At Prague many Familyees of Jewes liued packed together in one little house, which makes not only their howses but their streetes to be very filthy, and theire Citty to be like Dunghill. Also they feede continually upon Onyons and Garlicke, so as he had neede first to breake his fast, and haue some good Oder in his hand, who will enter their Citty or haue Conference with any of them.

. . . they haue Authority yearley to chuse foure Judges among themselues, to rule them and Judge causes betweene them, but in cases betweene a Jewe and Christian they are determined by the Christian magistrate. The Authority of the cheefe Rabbi or Priest is very great among them. They punish Adultry by standing up to the Chinn in water a whole day. Theft with restitution and recompence of dommages, but Murther was unheard of among themselues.

They had no slaues bought with money or so borne, but after the manner of Christians the poore serued the rich for yearely wages.

. . . They tooke such oppressiue usury, as it seemed wonderfull the magistrate would suffer them so to devoure Christians; upon a pawne of gold or siluer they tooke a fourth part, and upon a pawne of Apparerell or stuffe they tooke halfe the principall for vse, and neuer lent without pawnes. Yea wheras the lawe of Germany allowes but fyue in the hundreth for a yeare, many Christians were so wicked as to extort the former vse in the name of Jewes, agreeing with a poore Jewe to bring them the pawnes and the money when it was repayd, and then giueing the Jewes some part of the vse, did retayne the rest for themselues.

. . . the Bryde among them vsed to sett in the Synagog vnder a rich cloth of State, and to giue her Fayth to her husband in the hands of the Rabby, confirming it by taking a Ringe, and to spende the rest of the day in feasting and daunsing, with the doores open for all Jewes or Christians that would enter, permitting imbraces but no kisses whyle they daunsed. They admitted diuorce for Barrenness, and many like causes, euen the smalest where both partyes consented. The Virgins maryed at 11 or 12 yeares and the young men at 15 or 16 yeares age to avoyde fornication, and if they had no Children the first or second yeare, there was no loue but continuall reproches betweene themselues and their Parents.

. . . At Prague the Jewes washed the dead body, and wrapt it in linnen, and buryed it the same day before the sunne sett, calling the people to the Funerall by the voyce of a Cryer passing through all the streets. The body being brought to the graue, the boyes did reade songes written upon the wall of the Churchyeard, bewayling the mortal condition of men, and confessing death to be the most iust punishment of sinne, which ended, the body was putt in the graue without any further Ceremony but only the laying of a greene Sodd vnder the head. Then they retorned to the sayd wall reading another song, praying God for Abrahams Isackes and Jacobs sake, not to permitt the diuill to kill men, and recommendinge to those Patriarkes in vehemnt wordes the afflicted State of their Posterity.

. . . The Synagoges had no bells, but the people were called together by the voyce of a Cryer passing through all the streets. Each synagoge had some 20 or 30 Rabbyes, with some 400 Dollars allowed to each of them for yearely stipend, but of these one was supreme, who hauing a greater stipend, had care of educating their Children, and of preaching, which he did with his head covered, sometymes in the language of the Germans, sometymes in the Hebrewe toung. The whole Congregation did singe alltogether.

. . . They had lampes burning by day in the Synagoge, to the honour of God only, and these were very fewe. The wemen came not into the Synagoge among men, but vnder the same Roof had their owne Synagoge and a doore to enter it, hauing windowes or narrowe Cleftes in the wall to heare the men singing, but themselues only did reade or mumble with a lowe voyce, and were otherwise silent.

. . . They whip themselues in the Synagoges, but more gently then the Papists, being content to weare out the rods upon the stones; hauing broken the lawe, they come to the Rabby to impose punishment on them, but make no particular confession of the Fact. They keepe duly all their old Feasts, and Fastinges, yet fast not at nights but only at noone, and are very Charitable in workes of Pitty more spetially in ransoming Captiue Jewes.

. . . At Prague they Circumcised their Children upon the eighth day, and this Circumcision they vse to the dead as to the liuing, but thincke it not necessary to Saluation, (as at their first coming out of Egipt they werte not Circumcised in the wilderness for forty years), the Covenant firme without the seale therof when it cannot be had. My selfe did see the Ceremonyes therof in this manner when the Chylde came neere to the Synagog, they raysed a clamour in the Hebrewe tounge; Blessed is he that commeth in the name of the Lord. At the dore, the women not permitted to enter, deliuered the Chylde to the Father, who caryed it to the

Alter, and then was a generall offering made with great emulation who shoulde carry the box of powder, who the salt, who the knife, as in England wee offer who shall haue the Brides gloues. Then the Chyldes linnen Clothes being opened, the Rabby cutt off his prepuce, and (with leaue be it related for clearing of the Ceremony) did with his mouth sucke the blood of his priuy part, and after drawing and spitting out of much blood, sprinckled a red powder upon the wounds. The prepuce he had at the first cutting cast into a guilt syluer bowle full of wyne, wherof the Rabby the Father and the Godfather did drincke, sprinckling some drops into the Chyldes mouth. Then the prepuce or fore-skinne was taken out, and putt into a box of salt to be buryed after in the Churchyearde. The Father helde the Chylde all this tyme in his Armes, and together with the God Gather testifyed that it was the seede of Abraham, and so gaue the name to it. This donne the Father carying the Chylde backe to the doore of the Synagoge, there deliuered it to the Nurse and wemen expecting it. Thje daughters witout vsing any Ceremony insteede of Circumcision, haue names giuen them by their parents at dinner or supper upon the eighth day among frends called to the Feast, after the singing of a Psalme.

[59] George Eliot visits the Ghetto in 1858; from *The Journals of George Eliot*, edited by Margaret Harris and Judith Johnson, London, 1998.

The most interesting things we saw were the Jewish burial-ground (the alter Friedhof) and the old Synagogue. The Friedhof is unique – with a wild growth of grass and shrubs and trees and a multitude of quaint tombs in all sorts of positions looking like the fragments of a great building, or as if they had been shaken by an earthquake. We saw a lovely dark eyed Jewish child here, which we were glad to kiss in all its dirt. Then came the sombre old synagogue with its smoked groins, and lamp for ever burning. An intelligent Jew was our cicerone and read us some Hebrew out of the precious old book of the Law.

[60] Franz Kafka in 1920 imagines that the newly built streets of Josefov are haunted by the spectre of the vanished ghetto; from *Conversations with Kafka* by Gustav Janouch, translated by Goronwy Rees, London, 1971.

The dark corners, mysterious little lanes, blind windows, filthy courtyards, noisy taverns and secluded bars still live within us. We walk along the broad streets of the new city but our gaze and steps are unsure. We tremble inside, as if we were walking through the old squalid lanes. The insalubrious old ghetto is more real for us than our new hygienic surroundings. We walk around the city as if in a dream; we ourselves are only phenomenon of the past.

[61] A visit to the Old Jewish Cemetery in the second half of the twentieth century; from *Utz* by Bruce Chatwin, London, 1988.

It was now early evening and we were sitting on a slatted seat in the Old Jewish Cemetery. Pigeons were burbling on the roof of the Klausen Synagogue. The sunbeams, falling through sycamores, lit up spirals of midges and landed on the mossy tombstones, which, heaped one upon the other, resembled seaweed-covered rocks at low-tide.

To our right, a party of American Hasids – pale, short-sighted youths in yarmulkes – were laying pebbles on the tomb of the Great Rabbi Loew. They posed for a photograph, with their backs to its scrolling headstone.

Utz told me how the original ghetto – that warren of secret passages and forgotten rooms so vividly described by Meyrink – had been replaced by apartment buildings after the slum clearances of the 1890s. The synagogues, the cemetery and the Old Town Hall were almost the only monuments to survive. These, he said, far from being destroyed by the Nazis, were spared to form a proposed Museum of Jewry, where Aryan tourists of the future would inspect the relics of a people as lost as the Aztecs or Hottentots.

THE NEW TOWN

Around Wenceslas Square

---

[62] A British author describes the importance of Wenceslas Square in Czech history, since the Czechoslovak Republic was proclaimed here in 1918; from *The Double Eagle* by Stephen Brooks, London, 1988.

From my room on Wenceslas Square all amenities were instantly available: restaurants and airline offices, the cafe of the Europa Hotel and the chic photographic gallery on Jungmannovo Square, ice cream sellers and sausage stands selling *klobasy* that seemed largely composed of pig tumors. It was, of course, Charles IV who laid out the half-mile-long Wenceslas Square – rectangle would be a more accurate term for it – though the horse market that originally occupied the space has mercifully disappeared. In recent years the square has been turned into a pedestrian precinct and the trams that once trundled up and down have been diverted elsewhere. Whenever the Czechs decide to scribble a footnote on the pages of European history, they usually do so here. The Republic was proclaimed here in 1918, Red Army tanks made a triumphal procession through the square in 1945, and after their return in 1968 the philosophy student Jan Palach incinerated himself in January 1969 not far from the statue of St Wenceslas which stands at the top of the square near the massive National Museum.

[63] An American roving reporter, Virginia Cowles, is based at the Ambassador Hotel during the tense days leading up to the Munich Crisis in September 1938; from *Looking for Trouble* by Virginia Cowles, London, 1942.

I arrived in Prague to find the capital chilled by an air of menace, with the centuries-old buildings looking sad and grey beneath an overcast sky. Everywhere there were signs of feverish activity; workmen were digging air-raid shelters in the park; women queueing up outside the shops to lay in stores of food; children being fitted with gas-masks. Thousands of civilian recruits with suitcases and bundles were streaming into the barracks, and all day long troop trains pulled slowly out of the station. Although there was an emergency censorship on the Press, extras appeared every few hours and were immediately sold out. The cafes were crowded with people in anxious speculation, and every now and then you overheard a grim snatch of conversation.

'To-night. Do you think the bombers will come to-night?'

Yet, in spite of this hourly uncertainty, life went on in its normal swing. That was what always struck one most in a crisis; the commonplace things that people did and said. Men having their hair cut, women arguing with the grocer, children going to the cinema. Even the porter in the Hotel Ambassador greeted me with a polite, matter-of-fact smile, and said, 'I'm glad to see you back' – as though I'd come for a holiday!

The hotel was already full of press correspondents, photographers and broadcasters. The telephones were ringing just as they had rung in Nuremberg, Paris, Berlin and London, ready to relay the latest news from Prague.

The Old Town Hall and the Church of Our Lady
before Týn in the mid-nineteenth century by A. Mathieu

A view of the Old Town Hall in the 1930s; photographer unknown

The Astronomical Clock (detail); photo by Jan Kaplan

The Old-New Synagogue and the Jewish Town Hall circa 1900 by V. Jansa

Wolfgang Amadeus Mozart (inset) and the former Nostitz (now the Estates Theatre) in 1830 by V. Morstadt

Hitler surveying Prague from the window of
Prague Castle on 16 March 1939

The Old Town Square in May 1945, photographer unknown

The Soviet Invasion of Czechoslovakia in August 1968; photo B. Hajný

Václav Havel in 1996; photo by Jan Kaplan

The Stalin monument by O. Švec – completed in 1955, demolished in 1962

I ran into Ed Beattie of the United Press, who had arrived that morning, and he told me that Knickerbocker and John Whitaker had gone into the Sudeten areas and were making their headquarters at Carlsbad. All sorts of reports were coming in about the fighting. The Germans were declaring it had turned into a bloody civil war and the Czechs were denying it. Ed and I decided to drive through the territory and find out for ourselves.

We hired a car and left the next morning. A few miles outside Prague we passed three school-children cycling down a dusty road, their pigtails flying in the breeze, with long grey cylindrical gas-masks slung carelessly over their handle-bars. A little farther on the Czech lines of defence started – neat rows of pill-boxes, camouflaged to look like haystacks, that stretched for miles across the fields. They were guarded by Czech soldiers with fixed bayonets and steel helmets, who seemed oddly out of place in the peaceful countryside; peasants in nearby fields went on working as though their presence was a matter of course.

[64] Graham Greene (staying at the Alcron Hotel) is, 'hoping to find himself in the middle of a revolution' during the Communist coup in February 1948; from *The Life of Graham Greene, Volume Two: 1939–1955* by Norman Sherry, London, 1994.

[*Greene*] thought of leaving Vienna by train because it would have been easier to reach Italy that way, but for the sake of adventure, he decided to fly: 'I suppose I could stop here & go down by train to Italy but that looks like missing an exciting story in Prague [a Communist Coup] & one's Catholic hosts might think one was turning tail.'

He arrived in Prague in the middle of a snowstorm. There was no food on the plane, no food in the hotel, and no rooms to be had. He spent the night on a sofa. Eventually, scrambling for food, he found his way to the basement, where he discovered a ball for the staff in progress and suddenly there was food aplenty. He watched the Venezuelan ambassador dancing with the fat cook (wise man) and felt, if this was a revolution, it was a happy one. Early the next morning he was in the streets seeking the blasts of riot and revolution to discover no more than a crackpot inventor who spoke of a parachute which could be guided for fifty kilometres after the drop, and, more extravagantly, a machine which could build a foot of wall every second.

Greene was in Prague for a week, still hoping to find himself in the middle of a revolution – but little was happening in the streets apart from marches and shouting crowds waving red flags. He remembered the novelist Egon Hostovský sitting on his sofa bed, and telling him that Jan Masaryk, the Czech Foreign Minister, had said goodbye to his staff and a few days later was dead, an apparent suicide which might well have been murder.

On 27th February 1948 a paragraph appeared in the *News Chronicle* about Greene the eternal traveller, under the heading of 'Czechmate': 'A guest in Prague's most ambitious hotel, the Alcron, when it passed yesterday from private into public ownership, was a novelist Graham Greene, who is in Prague at the moment to lecture for the British Council. He looked for his communist waiter. He had been appointed national administrator.' To which Greene replied when the note came to his attention: 'the Alcron did not pass from private into public ownership, I am certainly unaware of ever being served by a Communist waiter who had been appointed national administrator, and I was not lecturing for the British Council.'

The Emmaus Monastery Church

[65] A colourful Prague legend retold by a seventeenth-century traveller; from *Travels thro' Germany, Bohemia, Swisserland, Holland and other Parts of Europe* by Charles Patin, London, 1697.

The Spaniards have a Church in this City and consequently a Habitation with the title of Pilgrims of Emaus . . . The People are very devout . . . They show'd me in a Church the three Stones of a Pillar, which the Devil (as they say) had brought from Rome to deceive a certain Priest as he was celebrating Mass, with whom he had made a Compact. They added that St Peter threw this Fiend and his Pillar three several times into the Sea, and that this Balk having spoil'd all his Measures, he was so much enrag'd that he broke his Pillar for vexation, and nevertheless too fortunately found means to escape. My silence was not well interpreted by those related the Story to me, and I was obliged at last to declare whether I believ'd or not. I thought to have got off by saying, that I had never read nor so much as heard of it before, altho' I had been tolerably well informed of St Peter's Miracles, but that perhaps the circumstance of Time might afford me some light into the matter: Therefore I demanded of 'em when this happened; they answer'd many thousand years ago: I reply'd that the Christian tradition was establish'd only fifteen hundred years ago that is to say, since the Nativity of Jesus: It is true (said they) but the Miracle which we have mention'd to you is a great deal older than that: Thus my Chronologie being entirely subverted, I was almost forc'd to believe that the Catholic Church, St Peter and the Mass were much more ancient than they were supposed to be. In the same place I saw a large Stone tomb, which was found in Moldavia, with the body of St Antony. It is a considerable Monument, the Carving and Ornaments of which have a very great Conformity with the Sepulchres of the Primitive Christians that are discover'd in Italy.

. . . In the same Church is shown the Portraiture of the Virgin Mary, painted by St Luke; and I am only displeas'd to meet with these Pieces so often; for 'tis certain that People are mistaken as to the most part of 'em, it not being probable that St Luke ever drew so many Portraitures of the Virgin . . .

The Orthodox Cathedral of SS Cyril and Methodius

[66] On 18 June 1942 at 4.15 a.m. German troops surround the Church of SS Cyril and Methodius on Resslova Street – the hiding place of Reinhard Heydrich's assassins. Following a fierce gun battle inside the church the Nazis finally attack the crypt – the last redoubt of the three surviving Czechoslovak parachutists; from *The Assassination of Heydrich* by Miroslav Ivanov, London, 1973.

Dr Petřek took a step towards the hole, and said, 'I am ordered to tell you that you must surrender. Therefore I do so. And that nothing unpleasant will happen to you – that you will be treated as prisoners of war.'

Now for the first time voices were heard from below. 'We are Czechs! We shall never surrender: never, do you hear? Never! Never!'

[. . .] The SS officers called for volunteers. The group formed with no great haste. At first no one at all came forward; then after a fresh appeal a few men made up their minds and then the commanding officer picked the rest.

They were taken into the church. The Superintendent (of the Prague Gestapo) Pannwitz addressed them with a few well-chosen words. He spoke of the call of honour and showed them the black hole. A rope was brought; one end was put round a 'volunteer's' chest, and he was lowered into the hole. A howl of pain. He had been hit by the parachutists and had to be hauled out with a wounded leg. The hole was so narrow that it did not allow of the smallest movement.

The superintendent and the SS commander were completely at a loss: they saw they could lower one volunteer after another without achieving anything. And outside, in the street, K. H. Frank [*the Nazi Chief of Police*] was stamping up and down.

So now in their baffled fury they gave orders for the carpets to be rolled back and the whole floor of the nave examined. In a few minutes the ground was bare; one SS watched the hole and the others searched feverishly. Pannwitz hurried to and fro there must certainly be a way into the crypt – in former times the coffins of the monks had been laid there. How were the coffins taken down? There must be stairs, but where were they? Somewhere at the place where a stone sounded hollow. At last to their delight they found it, a heavy slab concealed beneath the altar.

The superintendent sent for the firemen and ordered them to break it. Behind them stood the SS, their rifles in their hands. But the slab held firm, and after twenty minutes a fireman tried to explain in pidgin German that it was impossible to deal with it with the tools they had there. The firemen were sent away and the SS ordered in with dynamite. They did something round the slab, then we were told to leave the church. They blasted the slab, and the heavy stone broke in two. An eager, inquisitive Gestapo man pulled away part of the wreckage and peered in to see what was inside – bullets whipped past his head. Pannwitz grinned with satisfaction: there were wooden steps leading into the crypt; this was the way down.

Once again the SS were called upon. They were to go down the steps, and this time they were sent group by group, in waves of attack.

How I admired those men in the crypt: for hours now they must have known that their struggle was hopeless, that sooner or later they would be killed; but they did not give in. They fought like lions.

The first SS attack failed. When they had gone a few steps down a burst of fire stopped them dead and some of them fell; they could not see clearly, and the stairs being so narrow and steep the wounded men threw the others into disorder. They had to retreat.

Meanwhile, in the street, a fireman was ordered to get hold of the ladder the besieged men used for pushing away the hoses. Frank wanted to flood them out – the fireman obeyed. He went along the wall of the church and just as a parachutist was thrusting at the hose he grasped the end of the ladder and pulled it out. K. H. Frank praised him, of course – it was a step nearer victory. They say that later the Nazis rewarded this fireman; and after the war a Czech court condemned him.

Now the parachutists' position was becoming critical. Water was flowing into the crypt and they no longer had anything to push the hose away with, for the little barred window was too high. At the same time the SS launched another attack, throwing grenades – and steadily the water flooded into the crypt.

Yet the parachutists went on firing. They hit back without a pause, resisting ferociously. How long could they hold out? Five minutes? Half an hour?

And then suddenly, at about noon, four isolated shots rang out below. After that, a great silence.

Pannwitz stiffened. He looked at the way into the crypt and beckoned to an SS officer. The SS hesitated, then sent two soldiers, who went cautiously down: one step, two steps, three. Still silence. They looked back at the officer, who waved them on. They moved down further still, everyone in the church watching them, hardly breathing. They vanished into the crypt and then called up: the officer hesitated no longer; with his revolver in his hand he rushed down. A moment later he reappeared, wet above the knees, and cried, 'Fertig!'

It was over.

OUTSIDE THE WALLS

The White Mountain
(Bílá Hora)

[67] After accepting the Bohemian crown, Frederic (the Winter King) and his consort Elizabeth arrive at the Star Palace on the White Mountain, on the morning of 31 October 1619.

An autumn haze lay over the White Mountain, and a heavy dew sparkled on the scant grass which clothed the long, bare slope. A train of splendid travellers wound its slow way along the road which leads out of far-off Germany to Prague. First clattered a regiment of mounted arquebusiers, whose accoutrements glittered bravely in the morning sun. Behind them came a gallant cortege of nobles, and following these were five guilded coaches. Then came a detachment of men-at-arms and a long file of baggage wagons and sumptermen with laden horses. This day Friedrich, King of Bohemia, and Her Majesty Queen Elizabeth, with their suite, journeyed from the Castle of Bustěhrad, where they had spent the preceding night, to their town of Prague.

Autumn had decked Bohemia to greet her new sovereign: the bare hills, so unutterably dreary under a leaden sky, smiled to-day beneath the haze, smiled and glistened in the morning dew.

Beside Her Majesty's coach rode my young Lord Bernard of Thurn, son of the statesman. The elder Thurn was a polished courtier, a man who knew both Court and camp; but, though he played the patriot, he was, in truth, more Austrian than Bohemian; whereas his son, brought up at Prague, was a true Czech, with all the Czech's fiery love of his country.

Bernard Thurn rode beside Elizabeth Stuart's carosse and told her, in glowing words, a dozen histories of old Bohemian days . . .

The sun was high in the heavens when the King's cortege drew near to the Star [*Summer Mansion*] Palace on the White Mountain, that quaint Renaissance pavilion which the Archduke Ferdinand of Austria had caused to be built for the Lady Philippine Welser, the patrician maiden of Augsburg, whom he had raised to royal rank by wedding her in the face of the Emperor's bitter hostility. A strange pavilion, this Star Palace, for even a hunting lodge in those days was perforce fortified, and the Palace, built in six massive-pointed sections to portray a star in stone, was surrounded by a ponderous loopholed wall; and it was believed that the Star Palace was an impregnable, if miniature, fortress.

That day the heavy gates stood wide open; Bohemia's flag flew bravely above the Palace; rich tapestries were hung from out the windows, and a crowd of gorgeously clad nobles stood before the door eager to greet their Sovereign Lord and his gracious Lady.

Right glad was this meeting between Friedrich of the Palatinate and the men who had made him King. The autumn sun shone on the scene enough, and surely it was of happy augury that the new King and Queen should make their entry into Prague on this smiling autumn day.

In the Star Palace a banquet had been spread, and soon the pavilion rang with laughter and young voices.

After the banquet the English ladies wandered with the Bohemian gallants through the quaint chambers formed by the six points of the star. Tapestries were hung on the walls beneath those delicate Renaissance mouldings of the frieze, which have made the Star Palace famous as a very treasury of perfect design. In each room logs flamed in the wide, open fireplaces; and the ladies vowed that Bohemia was a friendly land . . .

The Bohemians were hugely diverted by Her Majesty's monkey, and when she told them, in her light way, that he was her eldest son, they laughed long. Little Prince Hal, leaning against his mother's knee, cried out that he was her eldest son.

'Mother, I am Prince of Bohemia!' he whimpered angrily.

'Nay, sweeting, Jacky is my heir!' returned Elizabeth, laughing. A chill fell on the laughing group. The Bohemians found this a sorry jest. Did their new Queen mock them? Did she mean that a monkey was good enough to be Bohemia's King? The unfortunate are easily wounded by a light word, and the Bohemians, ever an unlucky race, are morbidly sensitive and quickly suspicious.

Elizabeth Stuart saw the changed look on the courtiers' faces. With a sudden sense of helplessness she realized that a foreign language is a dangerous vehicle for jest. She had spoken in French, and the Bohemians for the most part know the language but indifferently.

She glanced at the King. He was standing in the embrasure of one of the windows with Hohenlohe, old Thurn, and Master Scultetus. Affairs of State at the wrong moment, of course, she thought impatiently! She rose.

'We must hurry onwards now,' she cried. 'I would fain tarry at this happy place, but I am all impatient to behold my new abode in Prague.'

The bevy of English damsels gathered round her, the coaches were summoned, and amid laughter and gaiety the cortege resumed its way over the White Mountain.

When the travellers came to the brow of the hill, Prague lay like a dream-city in the haze of the autumn midday. The sun touched to splendour the myriad turrets, towers, cupolas, and spires of the Hradčany Palace, and the broad majestic Moldau [*Vltava*], sweeping grandly onwards between the 'Old City' and the 'Small Town,' seemed to be an inlet from the blue sky.

[68] The Battle of the White Mountain (8 November 1620); from *Wallenstein* by Francis Watson, London, 1938.

Through the summer of 1620 the Bohemian cause continued to give evidence of its fatal weaknesses. What the heroic Žižka ['*the Czech Cromwell*'] had been able to perform two centuries before with an untrained but determined peasantry, could not be accomplished by a directorate divided amongst itself, neither feeling nor inspiring confidence, and frantically buying help for which it could not pay. In foreign diplomacy scarcely a success was to be registered.

. . . When the [*Habsburg*] Imperial forces came before Pilsen, interrupting the march on Prague in order to deal first with Mansfeld, that ill-used commander concluded an armistice with them. His mercenaries had received no pay for a year. To these misfortunes must be added the entire ignorance of military matters of the new Bohemian sovereign. 'Never,' writes Count Lützow, 'was Bohemia less prepared to resist the vast forces now on the march against her.'

The irony of destiny chose for the decisive meeting the very ground on which, just a year before, the Bohemians had first paid homage to Frederick of the Palatinate. On the White Mountain outside Prague, close to the walled park of the Star [*Summer Mansion*], Christian of Anhalt occupied a strong position on the evening of November 7th. He had escaped a flanking movement and hurried to protect the capital, to which Frederick, after some ineffectual manoeuvres in the field, retired without his army.

Early next morning, which was a Sunday, the first of the Catholic troops appeared on the hill, led by Maximilian and his general Tilly. They were shortly joined by Bucquoy's Imperial Forces, among them Wallenstein's regiments, and although Bucquoy hesitated, incapacitated by a wound in the groin, Tilly's decision to attack carried the day.

The opposing forces stood roughly equal at about 27,000 men, but among the defenders was division and discontent. In a few hours it was over, the fate of the Bohemians and their allies decided, and their horse and foot flying headlong into Prague. Only in isolated instances was there any refusal to join in the general rout. Frederick's bodyguard from the Palatinate in their steel-blue armour, and a small party of Moravians who retreated to the wall of the park, died almost to a man in defence of a hopeless cause.

In Prague Frederick had attended morning service. Returning to the castle to a banquet in honour of the envoys of his father-in-law James I – in whose favour he appears even at this hour to have placed a pathetic trust – he met the fugitives pouring into the city. His goods must have been already packed for flight, for in a short time he too was crossing the Moldau bridge with his Queen and a train of baggage-wagons. In the Old Town on the right bank he waited, taking counsel with his advisers, most of whom (and among them Thurn and Anhalt) recommended the inglorious flight of all concerned.

The English envoys were persuaded to send a message to the Imperial camp, but no answer was returned. On the next morning it was decided that the Queen should leave at once with her young child [*Prince Rupert*], while Frederick remained in Prague. But when Elizabeth and the infant were seated in the carriage prepared for them, and about to take leave, his glimmer of resolution died within him. Leaping upon his horse he gave the signal for each man to trust to his heels. His wife, who had shown more fortitude than he, was at this time pregnant with her fifth child.

Thus ended, with the Battle of the White Mountain [*Bílá Hora*], the bid for Bohemian liberty that had begun so inauspiciously with the Defenestration of Prague. At one stroke Frederick lost both the kingdom of Bohemia and the German Palatinate, and his brief and luckless reign, from one November to the other, establishes him romantically in history as 'The Winter King.'

When news of the catastrophe reached England, thirty gentlemen of the Middle Temple incontinently knelt down and swore upon their swords to reconquer for the captivating Elizabeth the glory she had lost; and during the long and tragic exile in Holland which followed she was not without faithful friends.But neither she nor her husband ever saw Prague again.

The Ruzyně Prison

[69] The American author Marcia Davenport reports on the brutal Nazi treatment and murder of Czech students in November 1939; from *The Valley of Decision*, London, 1946.

Then Jindřich began to talk. The special miracle of his presence here was that the last any of them had heard of him was a rumour that he had been among the martyrs shot in the massacre of students in Prague six weeks ago . . .

'After they tortured Jan Opletal to death.'

'It was planned the way they plan everything,' Jindřich said in his strange new timberless voice.

'To the last signal. It was total, cold blooded massacre – only with Nazi refinements. Plain murder is too dull for them . . . They gave the signal with a rocket, precisely at half past three in the morning of November seventeenth. We were all asleep. They knew exactly where every student in Prague lived, who slept in dormitories, who in boarding houses and hostels and at home. They had surrounded every building and house with guns and tanks and loaded cannons and platoons of armed troops, and of course the specialists of the SS with their whips and truncheons. When the rocket went off they broke down the doors of every house simultaneously. If anybody tried to keep them out they shot them down. There was resistance at the Švehla Foundation so they opened fire and the place was strewn with corpses in pajamas. Some places they simply stamped and bayonetted the boys right in bed . . .'

'They had buses parked outside the buildings and they dragged the men and girls out, prodding them with bayonets, and drove them into the buses like cattle. Some had pulled on shirts and pants but many were still in pajamas. None of the girls were dressed . . .'

'There were thirty-one busloads,' he said . . .

'I was there,' Jindřich said.

'They drove the buses to Ruzyně. You know.' They all nodded. Ruzyně was the airport of Prague. Some of its fields were surrounded by hangars and others by the barracks of the air force. There was also a cavalry riding-school there.

'They stopped the buses and kicked and dragged everybody out and got to work without delay. They set up a circus in the riding-academy. Several SS-men stood in the middle with horsewhips and made the men run round the track hour after hour after hour, whipping them when they collapsed from exhaustion, until finally there were none left conscious any more. But that was fairly humane. While that was going on they had a special collection outside on the field, a lot of men who were marked for particular punishment because they had pictures of Masaryk and Beneš in their rooms. They ripped the pajamas off those chaps and knocked them down with their gun-butts and fists and truncheons and then to stand up. Most of them were badly injured to get up, so they brought them to by throwing the pails of cold water on them. It was freezing that night,' he said. 'But it was still rather humane. There were some fellows who had actually offered resistance when the dormitories were broken into. They had there rounded up for themselves. They tied them together in threes.' His thin hands were twisted tight on the

edge of the table in front of him. 'They gave the signal for a
free-for-all. Indiscriminate mutilation. Ears, eyes, noses,
tongues, fingernails, toenails – no holds barred. A lot of them
were castrated then and there . . .' 'There are no words to
tell you what it sounded like,' he said. 'The sight will come
back all the rest of my life, the eyes popping out, the blood
running down the legs, but the sound . . . Our fellows
were tough. But the laugh. The things those offal roared to
one another, the names they had in their stink of a language
for the things they did. The crack of whips. The sound of
bones breaking . . . teeth grinding. And the laughs' – he
leaned forward. 'They had some of their own dirt there –
stenographers and clerks sitting in the upper windows of
the barracks. At typewriters. Laughing and watching the
whole thing. A glorious gladiatorial show, free for nothing.'

'Yes, they took the girls too.' Claire and Anton
exchanged a look.

'All the girls.' He did not have the courage to mention
Dora's name.

'They pissed into spittoons from the offices and held
them up and made the girls –' Claire's hand went to her
mouth and Anton shot Jindřich a look of warning.

But in a moment Claire said coldly, 'Go on.'

'They drove up a lot of tanks and made a ring of them
on the landing field and tied some of us to the tanks, so we
would have to watch. Then they dragged the girls out into
the ring of tanks and stripped them naked and knocked
them flat on the ground and lined up and raped them.
Systematically, understand. Always they do everything with
system. So many to a girl. Standing them in a line, telling
each other it was a cold night for outdoor sport.'

'Christ!' It was a scream from Claire. But Jindřich
seemed not to notice the interruption.

'When the girls passed out,' he said in the same nerveless
voice, 'of course they gave them the ice water restorative.
Only some never came to. The little delicate ones.'

'There are no more students or places to study. But
you know all that. You know about the closing of the
schools. And what they've been doing to the professors and

teachers and doctors and writers and scientists. I guess you know all that.' He laughed in a deathly way. 'They think they've destroyed all the brains in the country now, or made them powerless. So they'll only have a pack of beast of burden to drive.'

The Holešovice Trade Fair Hall (The former Deportation Centre of the Prague Jews)

---

[70] In the autumn of 1941 the Germans begin the mass deportation of the Czech Jews from Nazi-occupied Prague; from *I Do Not Want To Remember* by Heda Margolius Kovály, London, 1973.

The mass deportations of Jews from Prague began in the autumn of 1941. We had been ordered to report for transport, with no idea of our destination. The order was simply to report to the Trade Fair Hall, with food for several days and essential baggage. No more. When I got up that morning, my mother turned away from the window and said, almost childlike, 'Look, the sun is rising. I thought not even the sun would rise today.' But it rose, and on the streetcar people around us rode to their jobs as if it were just another day.

The scene in the Trade Fair Hall overwhelmed us. Our nerves were stretched to the breaking point. Several of the severely ill, brought there on stretchers, died that morning. There were women screaming in sheer hysteria – a Mrs Tausig tore her dentures from her mouth and threw them at out lord and master, Obersturmbannfuhrer Fiedler. She raved for several hours until the sounds she made were no longer human. There were small children and babies, too, weeping ceaselessly, while next to us a short, fat man with a shiny bald head sat on his suitcase as if it all did not concern him, playing Beethoven's Concerto in D major on a violin, practicing the difficult passages over and over again.

I wandered about, searching out familiar faces among those thousand people. That is where I first saw him. To this day I think he was the handsomest man I ever saw. He sat upright, composed, on a black suitcase trimmed in silver, wearing a dark suit, a white shirt with a pearl grey tie, and a black overcoat.

He had a handsome black hat and was leaning on a stick-thin, tightly rolled umbrella. His eyes were grey, and so was his faultlessly trimmed beard. The hands folded on the handle of his umbrella were slender and well-groomed.

Amid the chaos of people bundled up in sweaters, heavy boots, and quilted jackets he stood out as if he were stark naked. I stopped before him, startled.

He rose, bowed with a smile and offered me a place on the suitcase next to him. He was a professor of classical philology from Vienna. When the Germans had overrun Austria, he had escaped to Prague, and there the Germans caught up with him. I asked him why he had not selected something a bit more practical for a journey to God knew where, but he replied that he had always dressed like this and did not like to change his habits under the pressure of circumstances. In any case, he considered it most important to retain equanimity *rebus in arduis*. Then he spoke of ancient Rome and classical literature. I sat there spellbound. Later, I went to see him whenever I got a chance, and he never failed to welcome me with that courteous smile and, it seemed, with pleasure.

Two days later we were put on a train. In the following years I lived through infinitely more cruel transports, but this trip still seems the worst, perhaps because it was the first. If every beginning is hard, the beginning of something hard is hardest.

Libeň
(The scene of the
assassination of
Reinhard Heydrich in 1942)

[71] Reinhard Heydrich was considered the most dangerous man in Nazi Germany after Hitler himself. The plot to kill him, masterminded in England, was carried through to finality in Prague in May 1942; from *The Assassination of Heydrich* by Miroslav Ivanov, London, 1973.

(Soon after the attack, which left Heydrich mortally wounded, a large poster printed in black on a red background appeared on walls around Prague. This is a particularly important document because it shows that the Nazis had succeeded in finding out details about the attack.)

ATTEMPT UPON THE
ACTING-REICHSPROTEKTOR'S LIFE*

Ten million crowns reward for all information leading to the arrest of the guilty men. At about 10.30 hours on 27 May 1942 an attempt on the life of the acting-Reichsprotektor, **SS Obergruppenführer Heydrich**, was committed. The acting-Reichsprotektor was travelling from Panenské Břežany by the Kirchmayer Boulevard and his car was turning to the right in V Holešovičkách Street, Prague Libeň, in order to reach the centre of the town. At this point a man stood in the roadway and endeavoured to open fire on the occupants of the car with a submachine gun. At the same time another man threw a bomb that exploded on touching the car. After the attack, one of the men ran away along the Kirchmayer Boulevard, Na Kolinské and Na Zápalci; there he entered František Brauner's butcher's shop at number 22. He fired several shots from the shop and then continued his flight along Na Zápalci and V Holešovičkách, probably towards the centre of the town. The other man made off on a bicycle towards Stará Libeň.

The second man, of average height, slim, and dressed in a dark brown or black suit, wore a black hat. [. . .]

1. Who can give information on the criminals?
2. Who noticed their presence at the place of the crime?
3. Who are the owners of the objects described, and above all, who has lost the woman's bicycle, the coat, the beret, and the briefcase described above?

These objects may be seen from 09.00 hours today onwards in the window of the Bat'a shoeshop at 6, Wenceslas Square, Prague II. Whoever is capable of providing the information called for and who does not come forward voluntarily to the police will be shot together with his family, according to the terms of the ordinance of 27 May 1942 on the proclamation of the state of siege.

All may be assured that their information will be treated as strictly confidential.

Furthermore, from 28 May 1942 onwards it is the duty of all owners of houses, flats, hotels, etc., to declare to the police the names of all persons in the whole Protectorate whose stay has not yet been registered at the police station. Disobedience to this regulation will be punished by death.

**Information is received by
the secret state police at the chief office in Prague
(Staatspolizeileitstelle Prag) at 20 Bredovska, Prague II,
telephone 200 41, or at any German or Protectorate
police station; and this information may be given by word
of mouth or by telephone.**

Prague, 28 May 1942.

**The SS Obergruppenführer and Chief of Police attached
to the Reichsprotektor in Bohemia and Moravia (*signed*)
K.H. Frank**

On Hitler's orders, K.H. Frank issued the following ordinance:

In the region of the Prague Oberlandrat, the state of siege is proclaimed by the reading of this ordinance on the radio.

The following measures are laid down: The civilian population, without exception, is forbidden to go into the streets from 21.00 hours until 06.00 hours.

All inns and restaurants, cinemas, theatres and places of amusement are to be strictly shut and all traffic on public highways is forbidden during the same period.

Any person who appears in the streets in spite of this prohibition shall be shot if he does not stop at the first summons.

Other measures are foreseen, and if necessary they will be announced on the radio.

[* *Heydrich died on 4 June at Prague's Bulovka hospital and was buried with full military honours in Berlin on 9 June. The following day, SS units under the command of Max Rostock attacked the village of Lidice.*]

Smíchov

[72] A young Czech artist in 1991 creates an overnight sensation using a few pots of pink paint and a disused Russian tank; from *The Pink Scarf* by Bohumil Hrabal, translated by James Naughton, London, 1995.

A few days ago, on the 28th April, David Černý, student of sculpture at the Prague School of Applied Arts, went over to Smíchov, to the Square of the Soviet Tank-Corps, and painted its green memorial tank a rosy pink. For, as he said to the journalists, pink is the colour of an infant babe in arms, a symbol of innocence . . . All day long onlookers flocked to see this unreal thing which had actually come to pass . . . Cameramen rushed, while there was yet time, to film this wondrous sight of Prague, which knocked Allan Kaprow's one-time happenings into a cocked hat . . . And it was some time before the army came to drape a green military tarpaulin over the pink tank . . . Policemen went into the School of Applied Arts, infringing sovereign academic soil, and all day long they subjected a female student to forensic examination, all because she wore pink boots. Later on the soldiers painted the pink tank green again. The things that go on here in Prague . . . I was only sorry they demolished Stalin's monument all those years ago . . . Can you imagine, Miss April, what a wondrous sight that would've been, if David Černý had used his pink paint on Stalin as well? . . . In one fell swoop this would've made Prague the world centre for pop-art.

Around Vyšehrad

[73] Thomas Carlyle describes three historically important sieges of Prague (1741–2); from *History of Friedrich II of Prussia called Frederick the Great* by Thomas Carlyle, London, 1858–1865.

THE SCALADE [*ESCALADE*] OF PRAG

November 19th–21st, 1741. The Three Belleisle Armies, Karl Albert's first, have, simultaneously enough for the case, arrived on three sides of Prag [*sic*]; and lie looking into it, – extremely uncertain what to do. To Comte de Saxe, to Schmettau, who is still here, the outlook of this grand Belleisle Army, standing shirtless, provisionless, grim winter at hand, long hundreds of miles from home or help, is in the highest degree questionable, though the others seem to make little of it: 'Fight the Grand-Duke when he comes,' say they; 'beat him, and –' 'or suppose, he won't fight? Or suppose, we are beaten by him?' answer Saxe and Schmettau, like men of knowledge, in the same boat with men of none. 'We have no strong place, or footing in this Country: what are we to do? Take Prag!' advises Comte de Saxe, with earnestness, day after day. 'Take Prag: but how?' answer they. 'By escalade, by surprise, and sword in hand,' answers he: 'Ogilvy their general has but 3,000, and is perhaps no wizard at his trade: we can do it, thus and thus, and then further thus; and I perceive we are a lost Army if we don't!' So counsels Maurice Comte de Saxe, brilliant, fervent in his military views; – and, before it is quite too late, Schmettau and he persuade Karl Albert, persuade Rutowsky chief of the Saxons; and Count Polastron, Gaisson or whatever subaltern Counts there are, of French type, have to accede, and be saved in spite of themselves. And so,

Saturday Night, 25th November 1741, brightest of moonshiny nights, our dispositions are all made: Several attacks, there if I remember; one of them false, under some Polastron, Gaisson, from the south side; a couple of them true, from the north-west and the south-east sides, under Maurice with his French, and Rutowsky with his Saxons, these two. And there is great marching 'on the side of the Karl-Thor (Charles-Gate)' where Rutowsky is; and by Count Maurice 'behind the Wischerad'; – and shortly after midnight the grand game begins. That French-Polastron attack, false, though with dreadful cannonade from the south, attracts poor Ogilvy with almost all his forces to that quarter; while the couple of Saxon Captains (Rutowsky not at once successful, Maurice with his French completely so) break-in – open Ogilvy from rearward, on the right flank and on the left; and ruin the poor man. Military readers will find the whole detail of it well given in Espagnac. Looser account is to be had in the Book they call Mauvillon's.

One thing I remember always: the bright moonlight; steeples of Prag towering serene in silvery silence, and on a sudden the wreaths of volcanic fire breaking-out all round them. The opposition was but trifling, null in some places, poor Ogilvy being nothing of a wizard, and his garrison very small. It fell chiefly on Rutowsky; who met it with creditable vigour, till relieved by the others. Comte Maurice, too, did a shifty thing. Circling round by the outside of the

Vischerad, by rural roads in the bright moonshine, he had
got to the Wall at last, hollow slope and sheer wall; and was
putting-to his scaling-ladders, – when, by ill luck, they
proved too short! Ten feet or so; hopelessly too short.
Casting his head round, Maurice notices the Gallows hard
by: 'There, see you, are a few short ladders: *mas enfans*,
bring me these, and we will splice with rope!' Supplemented
by the gallows, Maurice soon gets in, cuts-down the one
poor sentry; rushes to the Market-place, finds all his
Brothers rushing, embraces them with '*Victoire!*' and 'You
see I am eldest; bound to be foremost of you!' 'No point
in all the War made a finer blaze in the French imagination,
or figured better in the French gazettes, than this of the
Scalade of Prag, 25th November 1741. And surely it was
important to get hold of Prag; nevertheless, intrinsically
it is no great thing, but an opportune small thing, done by
the Comte de Saxe, in spite of such contradiction as we saw.'

THE RETREAT

Beyond the circuit of Prag, isolated in ten miles of burnt
country, Belleisle has no resource except what his own head
may furnish. The black landscape is getting powdered with
snow; one of the grimmest Winters, almost like that of
1740; Belleisle must see what he will do.

Belleisle knows secretly what he will do. Belleisle has
orders to come away from Prag; bring his Army off, and the
chivalry of France home to their afflicted friends. A thing
that would have been so feasible two months ago, while
Maillebois was still wriggling in the Pas of Caaden; but
which now borders on impossibility, if not reaches into it.
As a primary measure, Belleisle keeps those orders of his
rigorously secret.

Within the Garrison, or on the part of Lobkovitz, there
is a far other theory of Belleisle's intentions. Lobkovitz,
unable to exist in the black circuit, has retired beyond it,
and taken the eastern side of the Moldau [*Vltava*] as the
least ruined; leaving the Tolpatchery, under one Festititz, to
caracole round the black horizon on the west. Farther, as
the Moldau is rolling ice, and Lobkowitz is afraid of his

pontoons, he drags them out high and dry: 'Can be replaced in a day, when wanted.' In a day; yes, thinks Belleisle, but not in less than a day; – and proceeds now to the consummation. Detailed accounts exist, Belleisle's own Account (rapid, exact, loftily modest); here, compressing to the utmost, let us snatch hastily the main features.

On the 15th December 1742, Prag Gates are all shut: Enter if you like; but no outgate. Monseigneur le Maréchal intends to have a grand foraging tomorrow, on the southwestern side of Prag. Lobkowitz heard of it, in spite of the shut gates; for all Prag is against Belleisle, and does spy-work for Lobkowitz. 'Let him forage;' thought Lobkowitz; he will not grow rich by what he gathers;' and sat still, leaving his pontoons high and dry. So that Belleisle, on the afternoon of December 16th, – between 12 and 14,000 men, near 4,000 of them cavalry, with cannon, with provision-wagons, baggage-wagons, goods and chattels in mass, – has issued through the two South-eastern Gates; and finds himself fairly out of Prag. On the Pilsen road; about night-fall of the short winter day: earth all snow and '*verglass*', iron-glazed; huge olive-coloured curtains of the Dusk going down upon the Mountains ahead of him; shutting-in a scene wholly grim for Belleisle.

Brigadier Chevert, a distinguished and determined man, with some 4,000 sick, convalescent and half able, is left in Prag to man the works; the Maréchal has taken hostages, twenty Notabilities of Prag, and neglected no precaution. He means towards Eger . . .

FREDERICK THE GREAT CAPTURES PRAG

Wide wail in Bohemia that War is coming back. Nobility all making off, some to Vienna or the intermediate Towns lying thitherward, some to their Country-seats; all out of Prag. Willing mind on the part of the Common People; which the Government strains every nerve to make the most of. Here are fasts, processions, Prayers of Forty-Hours; here, as in Vienna and elsewhere. In Vienna was a Three-Days solemn Feast: the like in Prag, or better; with procession to the shrine of St Vitus, – little likely to help, I should fear. 'Rise, all fencible men,' exclaims the Government, – 'at last we will ballot, and make you rise:' – Militia people enter Prag to the extent of 10,000; like to avail little, one would fear. General Harsch, one of our ablest soldiers since Khevenhüller died, gets-in still in time; and thus increases the Garrison of regulars to 4,000, with a vigorous Captain to guide it. Old Count Ogilvy, the same whom Saxe surprised two years ago in the moonlight, snatching ladders from the gallows, – Ogilvy is again Commandant: but this time nominal mainly, and with better outlooks, Harsch being under him. In relays, 3,000 of the Militia-men dig and shovel night and day; repairing, perfecting the ramparts of the place. Then, as the provisions, endless corn is introduced, – farmers forced, the unwilling at the bayonet's point, to deliver-in their corn; much of it in sheaf, so that we have to thrash it in the market place, in the streets that are wide; and thus in Prag is heard the sound of flails, among the Militia-drums and so many other noises. With the great church-organs growling; and the bass and treble *Miserere* of the poor superstitious People rising, to St Vitus and others. In fact, it is a general dance of St Vitus, – except that of the flails, and Militia-men working at the ramparts, – mostly not leading anywhither.

And so they are all assembled about Prag, begirdling the poor City – Third Siege it had stood within these three years (since that moonlight November night in 1741); – and are only waiting for their heavy military to begin battering. The poor inhabitants, in spite of three sieges; the 10,000 raw Militia-men, mostly of Hungarian breed; the 4,000 regulars, and Harsch and old Ogilvy, are all disposed to do their best. Friedrich [*Frederick*] is naturally in haste to get hold of Prag. But he finds, on taking survey, that the sword-in-hand method is not now, as in 1742, feasible at all; that the place is in good posture of strength; and will need a hot battering to tear it open. Owing to that accident at Teschen, the siege-cannon are not yet come up: 'Build your batteries, your Moldau-bridges, your communications, till the cannon come; and beware of Bathyani meddling with your cannon by the road!'

Siege-cannon having at last come (September 8th), the batteries are all mounted: – on Wednesday 9th, late at night, the Artillery, 'in enormous quantity,' opens its dread throat; poor Prag is startled from its bed by torrents of shot, solid and shell, from three different quarters; and make haste to stand to its guns. From three different quarters; from Bubenetsch northward; from the Upland of St Lawrence (famed *Weissenberg*, or White-hill) [*White Mountain*] westward; and from the Ziscaberg eastward (Hill of Zisca, where iron Zisca posted himself on a grand occasion once), – which later is a broad long Hill, west end of it falling sheer over Prag; and on another point of it, highest point of all, the Praguers have a strong battery and works. The Prag guns otherwise are not too effectual; planted mostly on low ground. By much the best Prag battery is this of the Ziscaberg. And this, after two-days experience had of it, the Prussians determine to take on the morrow.

September 12th, Schwerin, who commands on that side, assaults accordingly with the due steadfastness and storm-fullness; throwing shells and balls by way of prelude. Friedrich, with some group of staff-officers and dignitaries, turn cannon on them. 'Disperse, *Ihr Herren*; have a care!' cried Friedrich; not himself much minding, so intent upon the Ziscaberg. And could have skipt indifferently over your cannon-balls ploughing the ground, – had not one fateful ball shattered-out the life of poor Prince Wilhelm; a good young Cousin of his, shot-down here at his hand. Doubtless a sharp moment for the King. Prince Margraf Wilhelm and a poor young page, there they lie dead; indifferent to the Ziscaberg and all coming wars of mankind . . .

Schwerin, with due steadfastness and stormfullness, after his prelude of bombshells, rushes-on double-quick; cannot be withstood; hurls-out the Praguers, and seizes their battery; a ruinous low to them. Their grand Zisca redoubt is gone, then: and two subsidiary small redoubts behind it withal, which the French had built, and named 'the magpie-nests (*nids à pie*);' these also were ours. And we overhang, from our Zisca Hill, the very roofs, as it were;

and there is nothing but a long bare curtain now in this quarter, ready to be battered in breach, and soon holed, if needful. It is not needful, – not quite. In the course of three days more, our Bubenetsch battery, of enormous power, has been so dilligent, it has set fire to the Watermill; burns irretrievably the Water-mill and still worse, the wooden Sluice of the Moldau; so that the river falls the everywhere wade-able pitch. And Governor Harsch perceives that all this quarter of the Town is open to any corner; – and, in fact, that he will have to get away, the best he can.

White flag accordingly (Tuesday 15th): 'Free withdrawal. To the Wischerad; won't you?' 'By no manner of means!' answers Friedrich. Bids Schwerin from his Ziscaberg make a hole or two in that 'curtain' opposite him; and gets ready for storm. Upon which Harsch, next morning, has to beat the chamade, and surrender Prisoner of War. And thus, Wednesday 16th, it is done: a siege of one week, no more, – after all that thrashing of grain, drilling of militia, and other spirited preparation . . . rag has to swear fealty to the Kaiser; and pay a ransom of 200,000l.' Drilled militia, regulars, Hungarians, about 16,000, – only that many of the Tolpatches contrived to whisk loose, – are marched prisoners to Glatz and other strong places. Prag City, with plenty of provision in it, is ours.

BEYOND PRAGUE

Bohemian Rhapsody

[74] A sixteenth-century English traveller visits Bohemia and Moravia in 1592; from *An Itinerary* by Fynes Moryson, 1617, London, 1907–1908.

My selfe and foure consorts hired a Coach for 14 dollars from Dresden to Prague. The first day we went three miles to Gottleben a Village, where we paid five Bohemian groshe, that is sixe white groshe each man for his dinner . . .

The second day we went two miles through stony Mountains, bearing not one tree, to Ansig a little City, where we paid for our breakfast foure Bohemian groshes . . . The third day we passed 2 miles to a village called Welber or Welberg, through fruitfull hils of corn without any wood, & there each man paid 5 Bohemian grosh for his dinner . . .

. . . In the beginning of the yeere, 1592. I tooke my journey from Prague to Nurnberg, being six daies journey. The first day after dinner, we went foure miles, partly through rocky Mountaines, partly through a fruitfull corne plaine, and lodged at Berawn, where a loafe of bread, worth two third parts of a Creitzer, was a big as a threepenny loafe in England; by reason of the abundance of corne in that Country. And heere each man paid for his supper fourteene Creitzer . . .

. . . Moravia is a pleasant Countrey, very fruitfull, and full of townes and villages; and wee came to Ostrenam, where I paied for my supper three grosh, for beere two, for my hors-meat foure and halfe . . .

Here we dined with the Preacher (or Minister) of the Towne, because the Hoste of the Inne was newly dead; and I paid for my dinner foure grosh, for beere one grosh, and for horse-meat two grosh . . . The tenth day in the morning we rode two miles and a halfe; through hils of corne, and many woods, to a village, not farre from Ulrich-kirke, and here I omitted my expence [. . .]

[75] An eighteenth-century English lady's impressions of Bohemia; from *Observations and Reflections* by Hester Lynch Piozzi, London, 1789.

Bohemia seems no badly-cultivated country; the ground undulates like many parts of Hertfordshire, and the property seems divided much in the same manner as about Dunstable; my head ran upon Lilly-hoo, when they shewed me the plains of Kolin.

Doctor Johnson was very angry with a gentleman at our house once, I well remember, for not being better company; and urged that he travelled into Bohemia, and seen Prague; – 'Surely,' added he, 'the man who has seen Prague might tell us something new and something strange, and not sit silent for want of matter to put to his lips in motion!' *Horresco referens*; – I have now been at Prague as well as Doctor Fitzpatrick, but have brought away nothing interesting I fear . . .

[76] Thomas Carlyle's impressions of Bohemia in 1858; from *Carlyle* by David Alec Wilson, London, 1929.

Crossing into Bohemia [*on the way from Breslau on 12 September*] Carlyle reported: 'Our drive was as beautiful

as I ever had.' Taking train to Pardubitz, they found themselves among a crowd of 'dirty, smoking, Sunday gents, as
ugly on the Elbe as on the Thames.

'. . . The gents, that night led us to a place called
Pardubitz [*Pardubice*] . . . where one of the detestablest
nights of all this Expedition was provided me. Big noisy
inn, full of evil smells; contemptible little wicked village;
where a *worse* than gin-shop close over the way raged like
Bedlam or Erebus, – to cheer one in a "bed" 18 inches too
short, and matress *forced* into it, which cocked up at both
ends, as if you had been lying in the trough of a saddle: *Ach
Himmel*! We left it at 4 a.m. to do the hardest day of any:
Chotusitz and Kolin; such a day: in a wicked vehicle, with
spavined horse, amid clouds of dust under a blazing sun.'

. . . They reached Prague that night. 'This is a grand
picturesque town, this Prag,' [*Carlyle*] wrote to his wife,
enclosing a sprig of 'wild pink, plucked from the Battlefield
of Prag. Give it to some young lady who practises the
"Battle of Prague" on her piano to her satisfaction. . . .
Our journey from Prag [*the next day*] has excelled in confusion all I ever witnessed in this world; the beautifullest
country ever seen too, and the beautifullest weather; but –
Ach Gott!'

MUSIC IN PRAGUE

[77] Wolfgang Amadeus Mozart writes to Baron Gottfried von Jacquin from Prague, 25 October 1787; from *Mozart's Letters*, translated by Emily Anderson, London, 1990.

Dearest Friend!
You probably think that my opera is over by now. If so, you are a little mistaken. In the first place, the stage personnel here are not as smart as those in Vienna, when it comes to mastering an opera of this kind in a very short time. Secondly, I found on my arrival that so few preparations and arrangements had been made that it would have been absolutely impossible to produce it on the 14th, that is, yesterday. So yesterday my 'Figaro' was performed in a fully lighted theatre and I myself conducted.

In this connexion I have a good joke to tell you. A few of the leading ladies here, and in particular one very high and mighty one, were kind enough to find it very ridiculous, unsuitable, and Heaven knows what else that the Princess should be entertained with a performance of Figaro, the 'Crazy Day', as the management were pleased to call it. It never occurred to them that no opera in the world, unless it is written specially for it, can be exactly suitable for such an occasion and that therefore it was of absolutely no consequence whether this or that opera were given, provided that it was a good opera and one which the Princess did not know; and 'Figaro' at least fulfilled this last condition. In short by her persuasive tongue the ringleader brought things to such a pitch that the government forbade the impresario to produce this opera on that night. So she was triumphant! 'Ho *vinto*' she called out one evening from her box. No doubt she never suspected that the ho might be changed to a *sono*. But the following day Le Noble appeared, bearing a command from His Majesty to the effect that if the new opera could not be given, 'Figaro' was to be performed! My friend, if only you had seen the handsome, magnificent nose of this lady! Oh, it would have amused you as much as it did me! 'Don Giovanni' has now been fixed for the 24th.

October 21st. It was fixed for the 24th, but a further postponement has been caused by the illness of one of the singers. As the company is so small, the impresario is in a perpetual state of anxiety and has to spare his people as much as possible, lest some unexpected indisposition should plunge him into the most awkward of all situations, that of not being able to produce any show whatsoever!

So everything dawdles along here because the singers, who are lazy, refuse to rehearse on opera days and the manager, who is anxious and timid, will not force them. But what is this? – Is it possible? What vision meets my ears, what sound bombards my eyes? A letter from – I am almost rubbing my eyes sore – Why, it is – The devil take me 'God protect us' It actually is from you – indeed! If winter were not upon us, I would smash the stove in good earnest. But as I frequently use it now and intend to use it more often in future, you will allow me to express my surprise in a somewhat more moderate fashion and merely tell you in a few words that I am extraordinarily pleased to have news from you and your most precious family.

October 25th. To-day is the eleventh day that I have been scrawling this letter. You will see from this that my intentions are good. Whenever I can snatch a moment, I daub in another little piece. But indeed I cannot spend much time over it, because I am far too much at the disposal of other people and far too little at my own. I need hardly tell you, as we are such old friends, that this is not the kind of life I prefer.

My opera is to be performed for the first time next Monday, October 29th. You shall have an account of it from me a day or two later . . .

[78] A former British Ambassador to Prague, turned a musical sleuth, investigates the links between Mozart, Beethoven and the former proprietors of the Thun-Hohenstein Palace, now the British Embassy and ambassadorial residence in Prague; from *The Serpent and the Nightingale* by Sir Cecil Parrot, London, 1977.

Johann Joseph ('the old Count Thun'), was a friend and patron of Mozart, who was his guest on his first visit to Prague in 1787. The problem which I long tried to solve was where he actually stayed on this occasion. He wrote a letter from the Thun Palace to his friend von Jaquin about the Count and his orchestra, but, unfortunately, said next to nothing about the house. He was not really interested in buildings or beautiful objects, preferring people and society. We cannot be absolutely sure that the Thun Palace from which he wrote the letter was the British Embassy, because, at that time, there were at least five Thun palaces scattered all over Prague and three of them in the Malá Strana itself.

In addition to these palaces there was a house called the 'Thun *House*' in Sněmovní [*street*] which had once been joined to the present Embassy building. It is possible that guests of Mozart's status were housed in this particular building rather than in the palace itself, which for a 'palace' had rather modest dimensions. If this is true, and it is of course only conjecture, Mozart did not stay in the actual British Embassy building in Thunovská but in an outbuilding in another street.

More interesting than the Old Count Thun who died at the age of seventy-seven, a year after Mozart's visit, were his son and daughter-in-law, Franz Josef and Marie Wilhelmine Thun. Franz Josef was the founder of the Klášterec (Klosterle) branch of the Thuns. He was also a good friend of Mozart's, and his wife an even better one. She (formerly Countess Uhlfeld) did much for the musicians living at the time and is mentioned frequently in Mozart's letters. She had been a pupil of Haydn and 'having by chance discovered that Mozart was the composer of a sonata of great merit, she immediately appointed him her instructor on the pianoforte and in singing, though up to that hour he had been living in a garret and enduring extreme privations.' She was also a patron of Beethoven who dedicated one of his pianoforte trios to her. As one of the favourites of the Emperor Joseph, she did her best to persuade him that Mozart was a great pianist, and invited the composer to her home, when the Emperor was to be present as her guest. Mozart could not go and was 'half-desperate' because of it. He wrote of her: 'I have already dined twice with the Countess Thun, and go there almost every day . . . she is one of the most charming, lovely women I ever knew in my life – and I am in great esteem with her.'

When Mozart finally played before the Emperor, Countess Thun lent him her Stein piano, which was just as well, as, in Mozart's own words, 'the other piano was out of tune and had three of its keys sticking down.'

Her husband was a friend and disciple of Mesmer and acquired a reputation as a hypnotic healer. He was also a Rosicrucian and a freemason, which is interesting in view of the links between Rosicrucianism and freemasonry. Mozart was a freemason, as is well known from the masonic music he composed and the masonic symbolism of his opera *The Magic Flute*. But what is not so well known, is that the only noblemen on whom he called, when coming to Prague for the first time, were freemasons.

Count and Countess Franz Josef Thun had three daughters of great beauty, who were known as the 'Three Graces' and were also referred to in Mozart's letters. The eldest, Marie Elisabeth, married Count Razumovsky, the Russian Ambassador in Vienna, who commissioned Beethoven's 'Razumovsky' quartets. The second, Marie Christine, married Prince Karl Lichnovsky, who was a great friend of Beethoven and was often host to him in his castle at Hradec (Gratz) in northern Moravia. Beethoven dedicated his Second Symphony and Pathetique sonata to him. Lichnovsky was a patron of Mozart too and accompanied him on his tour of Prussia. The youngest of the 'Graces', Marie Caroline, married an Englishman Richard Meade, Earl of Clanwilliam. Their direct descendant is Flavia, Lady Ebbisham, whom I had the pleasure of taking round the Thun Palace, while it was being reconstructed.

The palace we were living in thus held many precious memories – if no tangible memorials – of the greatest musicians, and I would imagine them playing in that lovely suite of rooms under the light of the chandeliers, and reflected in the countless mirrors.

[79] In the 1870s, despite a sudden onset of the final stages of his fatal disease, Bedřich Smetana composes his most famous symphonic poems; from *Smetana* by Brian Large, London, 1970.

On October 20, 1874, a veil fell abruptly over Smetana's activities – activities which had completely revitalized Prague's artistic life and laid the foundations of modern Czech music.

Now fifty, he was quite deaf. He suffered continual pain, with the same rushing in the ears which had tormented him in the preceding weeks. An ether dressing applied through tubes failed to ease his state:

> I am to stay at home for almost a week. I cannot go out and have my ears wrapped in cotton wool since I must have complete quiet. I fear the worst – that I will become permanently deaf. I can hear nothing at all. How long will this last? If only I could be healed! And what if I do not get better?'

He could distinguish neither word nor note, even with an ear trumpet, and his family and close friends could communicate only in writing. His doctor experimented with a number of treatments, including the insertion of small tubes into the nostrils, which permitted air to be inhaled more directly. But this therapy was ineffectual:

> My ear infection is now as it was at the beginning of the month. I hear nothing in either right or left sides. Dr Zoufal still has hope but I despair! If only the rushing would stop!

The rushing never did stop. According to a letter written on December 11, 1881 to J. Finch Thorne in Tasmania,

> . . . it remains until now and continues day and night without ceasing. It is even stronger when my head is active and less noticeable when I am quiet. When I compose it is always in evidence.

Despite these pitiful entries he was able to work, and on November 18 recorded the completion of his symphonic poem Vyšehrad begun at the end of September. Two days later he took up his pen again, this time on a second tone poem, 'Vltava' (The Moldau). At one of the saddest periods of his life he managed to overcome adversity and misfortune, concentrating his creative powers to celebrate, in 'Má Vlast' (My Country), the glories of Bohemia. In this cycle he transforms shadows of personal darkness and misery to a paean of praise.

[80] In 1945 Sir Cecil Parrot attends a gala performance of Bedřich Smetana's opera *Libuše* at the National Theatre; from *The Serpent and the Nightingale*, London, 1977.

Not long after my arrival, I went along to the reopened National Theatre. The opera to be performed that night was Smetana's *The Libuše*. The theatre's motto was 'The Nation to Itself', and now once more it was able to resume the role for which it had been destined.

The occupation and dismemberment of the country by Nazi Germany in March 1939 had aroused an upsurge of national feeling among Czechs, who stretched out defenceless arms in the desperate hope of preserving what still remained of their sacred national heritage. Thus in the early summer of that year, the 'Musical May', as the Prague Spring musical festival used to be called, was turned into a national 'manifestation'. Under the baton of Talich, the great Czech conductor, the performance of Smetana's tone poem *My Country* [*Má Vlast*] and his opera *Libuše* evoked a deep, heartfelt response. Never was a nation so much at one. From that moment Czech national music was inevitably suspect in Nazi eyes.

When the liberation came in May 1945 and the government and most of the exiles had returned from abroad, it was with thankfulness and emotion that the nation celebrated its newly won freedom by producing operas which had been forbidden under the Nazi occupation.

At the opera there was a very representative audience including President Beneš and members of his government and the Diplomatic Corps. This opera has one notable feature. In its closing scene Prague's founder, Libuše, who according to legend was chosen by the Czech people as their judge because she had the power of soothsaying, prophesies a great future for her city. But she warns her people that they will have to go through many trials and tribulations. The climax of the opera is Libuše's unforgettable invocation, sung fortissimo: 'My dear Czech people shall never die. They shall gloriously overcome the horrors of hell.'

I did not know all this at the time and when we reached this passage I was rather startled to find that the whole audience, including the President, was suddenly standing up. At first I thought that the President had to leave early, although it struck me as curious that he should be doing so at this point in the performance. The truth was that it was an occasion of the greatest solemnity. *Libuše* was their most national opera, composed by their most national composer, and having so often in their history – and so very recently-faced the 'horrors of hell', they all rose instinctively in a prayer of thanksgiving for their deliverance.

[81] The shooting of a *Don Giovanni* sequence turns location filming for *Amadeus* into a slapstick comedy; from *Turnaround* by Miloš Forman and Jan Novák, London, 1994.

The most dramatic incident of our shoot occurred in the Tyl Theatre [since renamed the Estates Theatre], a very old and historical establishment that showed every year of its age. I wanted to film the excerpt from *Don Giovanni* there, as that was where it premiered, but the Czechs were reluctant to rent it to us, even though it was still a working institution. I understood their scruples once I inspected the backstage. It was in catastrophic condition, full of cobwebs and dust, old junk and rotted wood. The place was a powder keg and we were lighting our scenes with candles and torches as period authenticity dictated, so we told the Czechs we would pay for as many firemen as, in their judgment, it would take to safeguard the building.

We wound up with firemen crouching behind every stick of decoration on the stage, in every section of box seat, in every hallway. I think we had some hundred fire fighters on the set, but we almost managed to send the historical landmark up in flames anyway.

It was not for lack of caution. We wouldn't light the thousands of candles in the period chandeliers and candlesticks during rehearsals. Replacing all the candles took too long anyway, so we planned to ignite them only when we got ready to roll the camera.

Our first run-through of the dramatic master shot in which Don Giovanni confronts the black-masked ghost went very smoothly. The singer portraying the Don mimicked the words to the majestic sounds of our prerecorded music, and he looked splendid in his hat, adorned with peacock feathers. He was supposed to encounter the ghost, stagger, steady himself by leaning against a table on which stood a beautiful candelabra, and launch into his music.

I sat by the camera in the orchestra and watched. Everything looked fine to me, so I gave the order to light the candles.

With the playback booming, Don Giovanni saw the ghost, staggered, and caught himself from falling backwards by grasping the table. He had done everything precisely the way we had rehearsed it, but now the candles were burning up and the long feathers of his hat hung directly over the flickering candelabra. I froze as the peacock feathers began to smoke. A moment passed, then another, then another, as in a bad dream. The theatre was crawling with firemen, so I waited for them to spring into action. The feathers were now sprouting tiny flames and I watched and waited, but nothing happened. Don Giovanni went on mimicking the words with grand passion, not realizing that his plumes burned with big bright flames.

Where the hell were all the firemen?

It took another eternity of waiting before one fireman peeked out of the scenery. He was young and shy, and he flashed me an apologetic smile.

'Mr. Forman?', he said timidly. 'I am sorry, sir, but could you please stop the cameras? Your actor here is on fire.' And quickly he popped back behind the set, so that he wouldn't ruin the shot.

I've never seen a greater tribute to the magic of the movies. A couple of steps away from this fireman a man was on fire in a powder keg, but the camera was rolling so he didn't dare interrupt the movie.

'Cut!' I shouted when I realized the fire fighting was up to me. 'Cut! Cut! Cut!'

At that moment, a swarm of hollering fire fighters leaped out of the set decorations and threw themselves on the poor, unsuspecting Don Giovanni, knocked the elegant hat off his hat, and proceeded to stomp on it furiously. It looked like as if a Mel Brooks movie had suddenly erupted on the set.

[82] Three musical performances in Prague after the Velvet Revolution of 1989 make a strong impression on a Welsh travel writer; from *Fifty Years of Europe: An Album* by Jan Morris, London, 1997.

In the last decade of the century Prague became one of the great tourist destinations of Europe. It had tried to be one under the Communists, but in those days its drably printed brochures and smudgy programmes did little to counteract the dark reputation of the place, and not many foreigners responded. Now thousands came, and loved it – its buildings, its atmosphere, its beer, and perhaps most of all its music. When I was last in Prague I went to three musical performances which profoundly affected me in different ways.

The first was an impromptu jazz concert in Old Town Square, where that right-wing demagogue had said his piece. Throughout eastern Europe jazz had played an important part, almost a symbolic part, in the various risings which had put an end to Communism, and I thought it stirring to hear the blast of the saxophone, the wail of the blues, there in the heart of Prague. I sat drinking *borivicka* then, as the Good Soldier would have done before me, and Prague's glorious baroque skyline was silhouetted around me against a velvet sky. The horses of the pleasure-barouches stood chomping at their bits, attended by grooms in long cloaks and brown bowler hats; the performers played with immense ebullience; every now and then excited small children, encouraged by their fond parents, ran out to deposit coins in the band-leader's open trumpet-case.

My second performance gave me less benign sensa-tions. One windy morning I chanced to arrive at the gates of Hradčany Castle, beneath the proud standard of the President of the Republic, just in time for the changing of the guard. This struck me as an ambivalent display. The soldiers, in their long grey greatcoats, wore white scarves like Americans but marched like Russians. The bandsmen appeared at open first-floor windows, rather like the holy figures appearing at that very moment in the little windows of medieval clocks all over Europe, and they played a series of lush fanfares that sounded bathetically like film music. The flag flapped heavily in the wind above us. The troops marched and countermarched. The filmic fanfares sounded. I could imagine it all turning rather nasty if ever history started up again in Prague.

And my third concert was a recital, in the battered gilded church of Our Lady of Týn, of six different settings of Ave Maria (Schubert, César Franck, Cherubim, Saint-Saëns, Verdi, Gounod). It was extremely cold in the church, and we were all bundled in our pews. The soloist, Zdena Kloubová of the National Opera, sang from the organ loft behind us, and now and then I turned to see her. She looked very small and brave up there – almost defiant. She was wearing a black leather jerkin against the cold, and as her lovely voice rang out among the altars I thought her a haunting reminder of more heroic days among the Czechs: bad times, cruel times, but times when history happened.

PRAGUE LIFE,
CUSTOMS, MORALS

Eating and Drinking

[83] Pickled English oysters served in a Czech inn greatly surprise a sixteenth-century traveller from England; from *An Itinerary* by Fynes Moryson, 1617, London, 1907–1908.

In publike Innes they demand some six Bohemian grosh for a meale, yet doe they not commonly give meales at an ordinary rate, as they doe through all Germany; but what meate you require, that they dresse, and the servant buying all things out of doores (after the manner of Poland) maketh a reckoning of the expences. My selfe had my diet with a Citizen very conveniently for a doller and halfe weekely. I did here eat English Oysters pickled, and a young Bohemian coming in by chance and tasting them, but not knowing the price, desired the Merchant to give him a dish at his charge, which contained some twenty Oysters, and finding them very savoury, he called for five dishes one after another, for which the Merchant demanded and had of him five dollars, the dearenesse no lesse displeasing his minde, then the meate had pleased his taste.

[84] A banquet for the Turkish ambassador given by King Frederick's officials in 1620; from *A History of Bohemian Literature* by Francis Lützow, London, 1937.

Some of the officers of King Frederick, Bohemians of the Utraquist Church, gave in the evening a banquet to the Turkish ambassador, and among them was Henry Mathew, Count Thurn. The envoys of the Prince of Transylvania were also present, and of others Bohuchval of Berka, master of ceremonies; . . . (and) Peter Miller, vice-chancellor of the Bohemian kingdom . . .

The Turkish ambassador, holding a glass of wine in his hand, drank it to the health of Berka, begging him to consider him as his son, for both alive and dead, he said, he would be an obedient son to him. Berka gave as answer that he did not consider himself as being worthy that the ambassador and envoy of the great and powerful Turkish emperor should accept him as his father, he would rather wish to be his (the ambassador's) willing servant and menial. The Turkish ambassador accepted this, and answered further, that he was a Turk by birth and would die as such; he however, firmly and certainly thought that those who believed in Christ will be redeemed, even though they differed in opinion among themselves. Of the Emperor (of Austria) Ferdinand, however, he did not believe that he would be redeemed, for he had been the cause that the blood of many innocent people had been shed and of their destruction. He therefore thought that the devil would fry (Ferdinand) on a spit in hell.

Berka then declared that the House of Austria had always been the ruin of Bohemia, because [*with*] false Spanish practices it has sold the kingdom, his beloved fatherland, into perpetual servitude and made slaves of the Bohemians. Therefore the kind Lord God would not allow this any longer, nor permit that such tyranny and cruelty should be practised against them; but He in His great mercy had opened their eyes, and they had therefore taken up arms against Ferdinand and began war against the House of Austria. And rather than succumb to Spanish tyranny they would a thousand times rather submit to the rule and government of the Turkish emperor . . .

Peter Miller, the vice-chancellor of the Bohemian kingdom, said . . . 'We Bohemians have resolved, rather than that the Emperor Ferdinand should be our king – and supposing that the Turkish emperor is not able to help us sufficiently – we will seek refuge with the devil in hell and supplicate him to help us.'

. . . Then (Count) Thurn ordered three small glasses of wine and one larger glass that was empty, and said, addressing the Turkish ambassador: 'I drink these three glasses with you, one to the health of his Majesty the Emperor (of Turkey), one to the health of our own gracious King (Frederic) and one to that of the Prince of Transylvania.' And raising the three glasses he poured their contents into a large empty glass, and then continued: 'As with wine mixed out of three glasses it cannot be known what wine was in the first, what in the second, and what in the third glass, and only one sort of wine appears in this full glass . . . in the hope that these three potentates to whose health I am drinking will be of one accord, of one heart, and of one will; so that they may triumph over and defeat all their enemies.' Then he emptied the full glass of wine.

[85] In the late eighteenth century, Mrs Hester Lynch Piozzi finds the choice of culinary delights on offer in Prague quite outstanding; from *Observations and Reflections*, London, 1789.

The eating here is incomparable; I never saw such poultry even in London or Bath, and there is a plenty of game that amazes one; no inn so wretched but you have a pheasant for your supper, and often partridge soup. The fish is carried about the streets in so elegant a style it tempts one; a very large round bathing-tub, as we should call it, set barrow-wise on two not very low wheels, is easily pushed by one man, though full of the most pellucid water, in which carp, tench, and eels, are all leaping alive, to a size and perfection I am ashamed to relate; but the tench of four and five pounds weight have a richness and flavour one had no notion of till we arrived in Vienna, and they are the same here.

[86] An English author describes an unusual cure for Pilsner beer addiction in *fin de siècle* Prague; from *Three Men on a Bummel* by Jerome K. Jerome, London, 1900.

A suggestion of onions has clung to this tour since we left Prague. George has noticed it himself. He attributes it to the prevalence of garlic in European cooking.

It was in Prague that Harris and I did a kind and friendly thing to George. We had noticed for some time past that George was getting too fond of Pilsner beer. This Pilsner beer is an insidious drink, especially in hot weather; but it does not do to imbibe too freely of it. It does not get into your head, but after a time it spoils your waist.

. . . Now, I will drink no Pilsner beer. The white wine of the country, with a little soda-water; perhaps occasionally a glass of Ems or potash. But beer, never – or, at all events, hardly ever.

It is a good and useful resolution, which I recommend to all travellers. I only wish I could keep to it myself. George, although I urged him, refused to bind himself by any such hard and fast limit. He said that in moderation beer was good.

'One glass in the morning,' said George, 'one in the evening, or even two. That will do no harm to anyone.'

Maybe he was right. It was his half-dozen glasses that troubled Harris and myself.

'We ought to do something to stop it,' said Harris; 'it is becoming serious.'

'It's hereditary, so he has explained to me,' I answered. 'It seems his family have always been thirsty.'

'There is Apollinaris water,' replied Harris, 'which, I believe, with a little lemon squeezed into it, is practically harmless. What I am thinking about is his figure. He will lose all his natural elegance.'

We talked the matter over, and, Providence aiding us, we fixed upon a plan. For the ornamentation of the town a new statue had just been cast. I forget of whom it was a statue. I only remember that in the essentials it was the usual sort of street statue, representing the usual sort of gentleman, with the usual stiff neck, riding the usual sort of horse – the horse that always walks on its hind legs, keeping its front paws for beating time. But in detail it possessed individuality. Instead of the usual sword or baton, the man was holding, stretched out in his hand, his own plumed hat; and the horse, instead of the usual waterfall for a tail, possessed a somewhat attenuated appendage that somehow appeared out of keeping with his ostentatious behaviour. One felt that a horse with a tail like that would not have pranced so much.

It stood in a small square not far from the farther end of the Karlsbriicke, but it stood there only temporarily. Before deciding finally where to fix it, the town authorities had resolved, very sensibly, to judge by practical test where it would look best. Accordingly, they had made three rough copies of the statue mere wooden profiles, things that would not bear looking at closely, but which, viewed from a little distance, produced all the effect that was necessary. One of these they had set up at the approach to the Franz-Josefsbriicke, a second stood in the open space behind the theatre, and the third in the centre of the Wenzelsplatz.

'If George is not in the secret of this thing,' said Harris – we were walking by ourselves for an hour, he having remained behind in the hotel to write a letter to his aunt – 'if he has not observed these statues, then by their aid we will make a better and a thinner man of him, and that this very evening.'

So during dinner we sounded him, judiciously; and finding him ignorant of the matter, we took him out, and led him by side streets to the place where stood the real statue. George was for looking at it and passing on, as is his way with statues, but we insisted on his pulling up and viewing the thing conscientiously. We walked him round that statue four times, and showed it to him from every possible point of view. I think, on the whole, we rather bored him with the thing, but our object was to impress it upon him. We told him the history of the man who rode upon the horse, the name of the artist who had made the statue, how much it weighed, how much it measured. We worked that statue into his system. By the time we had done with him he knew more about that statue, for the time being, than he knew about anything else. We soaked him in that statue, and only let him go at last on the condition that he would come again with us in the morning, when we could all see it better, and *for* such purpose we saw to it that he made a note in his pocket-book of the place where the statue stood.

Then we accompanied him to his favourite beer hall, and sat beside him, telling him anecdotes of men who, unaccustomed to Pilsner beer, and drinking too much of it, had gone mad and developed homicidal mania; of men who had died young through drinking Pilsner beer; of lovers that Pilsner beer had been the means of parting for ever from beautiful girls.

At ten o'clock we started to walk back to the hotel. It was a stormy-looking night, with heavy clouds drifting over a light moon. Harris said 'We won't go back the same way we came, we'll walk back by the river. It is lovely in the moonlight.'

Harris told a sad history, as we walked, about a man he once knew, who is now in a home for harmless imbeciles. He said he recalled the story because it was on just such another night as this that he was walking with that man the very last time he ever saw the poor fellow. 'They were strolling down the Thames Embankment,' Harris said, and the man frightened him then by persisting that he saw the statue of the Duke of Wellington at the corner of Westminster Bridge, when, as everybody knows, it stands in Piccadilly.

It was at this exact instant that we came in sight of the first of these wooden copies. It occupied the centre of a small, railed-in square a little above us on the opposite side of the way. George suddenly stood still and leant against the wall of the quay.

'What's the matter?' I said. 'Feeling giddy ?'

He said: 'I do, a little.'

'Let's rest here a moment.'

He stood there with his eyes glued to the thing.

He said, speaking huskily: 'Talking of statues, what always strikes me is how very much one statue is like another statue.'

Harris said: 'I cannot agree with you there – pictures, if you like. Some pictures are very like other pictures, but with a statue there is always something distinctive. Take that statue we saw early in the evening,' continued Harris, 'before we went into the concert hall. It represented a man sitting on a horse. In Prague you will see other statues of men on horses, but nothing at all like that one.'

'Yes they are,' said George; 'they are all alike. It's always the same horse, and it's always the same man. They are all exactly alike. It's idiotic nonsense to say they are not.' He appeared to be angry with Harris.

'What makes you think so?' I asked.

'What makes me think so?' retorted George, now turning upon me.

'Why, look at that damned thing over there!'

I said: 'What damned thing?'

'Why, that thing,' said George; 'look at it! There is the same one.'

'How many copies of that statue did you say we saw?' asked George, after we had finished.

'Three,' replied Harris.

'Only three?' said George.

'Are you sure?'

'Positive,' replied Harris.

'Why?'

'Oh, nothing!' answered George.

But I don't think he quite believed Harris.

[87] Marcia Davenport observes the German soldiers hungrily 'stuffing their maws' with Czech food after the Nazi occupation of Prague in 1939; from *The Valley of Decision*, London, 1946.

Late in the evening they went back to town because Claire wanted to see who was at the [*Hotel*] Ambassador and what they knew. There was absolute censorship already, no use to try to send anything out, but the correspondents would still be about. The place was a madhouse as it had been during Munich, and now the city was afflicted with a new degeneracy. At the termination of the march the invaders had broken ranks and the soldiers were turned free. They fell upon the city, a horde of gluttonous locusts. Storekeepers were to keep their shops open. In every street there were wrangles and riots as the Germans lined up at the counters of shops and the tables of restaurants, buying (with phony money), gourmandising, stuffing their maws with goose and pork and pastry and chocolate and hunks of delicate pink ham and fistfuls of whipped cream and quarts of Plzeň beer and rivers of good honest coffee the likes of which some of them had never smelled, slapping together bars of candy, slabs of butter, whole sausages, layers of cheese, ramming the stuff down their throats and swilling everything good to drink after it. Claire was green with disgust, clinging silently to Anton's arm, as they made their way through the mobs on the streets and finally by inches, trampled and shoved, into the lobby of the Ambassador.

[88] In the early 1960s the narrator of one of Len Deighton's famous spy thrillers visits, (in what those days was), a very popular Prague pub called 'The Three Ostriches' from *Funeral in Berlin* by Len Deighton, London, 1965.

If anyone ever decided to illustrate Hans Andersen with photographs he would start in Prague. The heights of the city are a fairy tale of spiky spires; Hradčany castle and the steeple of St Vitus stare down to where the fourteenth-century Karlův bridge tucks the Three Ostriches tavern under its arm before crossing the calm blue Vltava. The older parts of the city are a maze of tiny twisting streets illuminated by gas lights and so hilly that a careless driver can find himself tobogganing down steep stone steps. It was twilight and the city looked like a dusty Christmas tree.

I parked my hired Skoda car and walked back towards the Three Ostriches tavern. The steps were worn to a glassy smoothness and the inside was like something whittled three lessons before Pinocchio. The overhead beams were painted with red and green vine leaves and varnished with about five hundred years of tobacco smoke. A tiny radio balanced over the tiled stove was beating out 'Walking my baby back home' with enough violence to make the potted geraniums quiver. The tables were as crowded as a Stakhanovite work schedule and merry groups of men shouted for slivovice, borovička or Pilsner Urquell, and the waiters kept a tally of their progress by marking each man's beer-mat with strange pencil marks.

[89] A stressed Prague housewife cooks a meal for her family in the 1980s; from *How We Survived Communism And Even Laughed* by Slavenka Draculić, London, 1987.

Veronika's kitchen window looks out on to the backyard. It is in the old part of Prague – Staré Město – where the houses look like fortresses, with strong walls and small windows. The facade across from her is crumbling from damp. The window is wet with raindrops. In the semi-darkness of the kitchen, Veronika moves silently, slowly. She doesn't have to tell me anything – her story, I mean. I can easily read it in her attitude, her movements, her absentminded glancing look, and her silence. She is making farina dumplings for the beef soup: one whole egg, a pinch of salt, a little oil, and a cup of farina. She mixes it automatically (the secret of good dumplings is in the mixing); there is no need to concentrate on her movements, this is what she does every Saturday. Nobody is home, her two sons are out, her husband Jiří, too. I know it's him that she is thinking about – his absence, longer and longer every day. She doesn't want him to leave, even if she knows he has a lover. She doesn't have time during the week to cook; the kids eat at school, she and Jiří too. So on Saturday she goes to the open market and buys food, fresh meat or fish, maybe vegetables, depending on what there is to buy. Today she found kiwi for dessert. It was very expensive, but she bought it because it is Saturday and they will all eat together. For Saturday lunch she cooks meals that the kids like, that he likes . . . as if she is mixing some kind of magic potion that will keep her family together – at least for a while, at least around the table. It takes a long time for the soup to cook, but finally she speaks to me. 'It's just that he is so unhappy, so frustrated. I understand him. In such a system I am happy to work as a little bureaucrat. But he is a journalist, and you know what kind of pressure they suffer. I don't know how I can help him – or us. Because if he leaves us, I feel like everything will fall apart, even these thick walls around me.' After the long silence, her words fall heavily, like the drops of rain outside.

Sex in Bohemia

---

[90] A seventeenth-century French physician Charles Patin encounters an early version of a Czech nudist camp; from, *Travels thro' Germany, Bohemia, Swisserland, Holland and other Parts of Europe*, London, 1697.

As we were passing between the River Elbe, and a small wood or copse, we were surpriz'd to behold at one end of the Meadows, as it were, an Epitome of the Ressurection, and of the last Judgment: For three and four hundred Persons suddenly rose up from the Ground on which they had lain: They took no care to dress themselves for want of Cloaths; not but the some few were meanly furnish'd with 'em, yet none had any sense of shame. I durst not describe what I saw, and much less what they proffer'd to shew me, in case I wou'd have bestow'd some small Benevolence upon'em. This was a Company, or if you please, a regiment of Bohemians, not of the Natives of Bohemia, but of those Bohemians by Profession, they have no trade, no Wealth, no Friends, and no Industry, and yet live, and that too with a sort of liberty, that you shall not meet with in the most free Republick in the World.

[91] In 1932 Hedy Lamarr, aged nineteen, shocks the world by faking an orgasm in the Czech film *Ecstasy*, filmed on location outside Prague in 1932; from *Ecstasy And Me*, London, 1966.

When I agreed to do the picture, there were no nude scenes, and no sexy close-ups. (Naïve sixteen! As I grew older, I learned how to make better deals for myself.)

The original script was a five-page affair, with hardly any dialogue. We were shooting (as it would be called today) 'off-the-cuff', in a forest lake outside Prague, when I baulked at the nude scene.

'Where is it in the script?'

The director shouted 'If you do not do this scene, the picture will be ruined, and we will collect our losses from you!' (Losses! I had a small salary, no percentage of anything, and never made a dime from the backers.)

We shot the other torrid love scene indoors.

I was told to lie down with my hands above my head while Aribert Mog whispered in my ear, and then kissed me in the most uninhibited fashion. I was not sure what my reactions would be, so when Aribert slipped down and out of camera, I just closed my eyes.

'No, No,' the director yelled. 'A passionate expression on the face.' He threw his hands up and slapped them against his sides. He mumbled about the stupidity of youth. He looked around and found a safety pin on a table. He picked it up, bent it almost straight, and approached. 'You will lie here,' he said, 'I will be underneath, out of camera range. When I prick you a little on your backside, you will bring your elbows together and you will *react*!'

I shrugged. Aribert took his place over me, and the scene began again. Aribert slipped down out of range on one side. From down out of range on the other side, the director jabbed that pin into my buttocks 'a little' and I *reacted*!

'No, No.' I had reacted in the wrong way. 'Elbows!' he yelled. So, several takes and jabs later, we were – getting nowhere. And now I shall quote an article from the Los Angeles *Herald-Examiner*, that appeared in the issue of January 28th, 1966.

> More than 250,000 feet was cut from *Ecstasy* before its release. These were love scenes reportedly so 'sizzling' that producer Josef Auerback called them 'too sexy' and ordered them burned. 'The love scenes were real,' Auerback said in a 1952 interview, 'since Hedy was engaged to her leading man at the time'.

So much for de Machaty and his pin; for Hedy Kiesler and her *reactions*; for Aribert Mog and his fiancée.

The truth is that some of those pinpricks shot pain through my body until it was vibrating in every nerve. I remember one shot when the close-up camera caught my face in a distortion of real agony, and the director yelled happily, 'Yes, good!'

Then again, Aribert had what would be called today 'Actors Studio' realism. But I have long resented his alleged cheap comments, as they show a complete ignorance of the creative process.

As I explained, there have been many versions of *Ecstasy*. These include revivals both illegitimate and 'legitimate' (including the use of clips in the United Artists 1964 feature *The Love Goddesses*). And there is continued talk about a new version. If you have ever seen *Ecstasy*, I can only say that in the close-up section, you *may* have seen me agonizing over pinpricks! And I have seen that section once myself in which the emotion on my face was pure *exhaustion*. Because there were takes when I just had nothing left, and could hardly focus my eyes.

In any case, *something* showed on the screen only too realistically, as I discovered at the preview.

By now, my parents were proud of me. Their little princess was a real movie star. We were in the best seats, and I was wearing a gown made for the occasion. The film began, and 'the' scenes approached.

'It's artistic,' I whispered to my parents nervously, when I could see right away that the forest was just too close! The next moment, I was running nude through the trees. Good lord, the camera seemed no more than twenty feet away! I felt my face turning crimson.

Remember, this was Europe over thirty years ago!

The swimming scene was quick, but not quick enough. They must have used a telescopic lens. As I sat there, I wanted to kill the director. Then, I wanted to run and hide.

My father solved the predicament. He simply rose, and said grimly, 'We will go.' I gathered my belongings in one grab. My mother seemed angry, but somehow reluctant to walk out. Nevertheless, walk out we did.

I was practically babbling about the telescopic lens. My father was talking furiously about indecent exposure. I was never to act in another picture. (Believe me, at that moment, I had no intention of doing so.)

It was a week before I dared to leave the house.

[92] In 1976, a New York writer attends a sex party at the seventeenth-century Campa palazzo; from *The Prague Orgy* by Phillip Roth, London, 1985.

At Klenek's every Tuesday night, with or without Klenek in residence, there is a wonderful party to go to. Klenek is currently directing a film in France. Because he is technically still married to a German baroness, he is by Czech law allowed to leave the country half of each year, ostensibly to be with her. The Czech film industry is no longer open to him, but he continues to live in his palazzo and is permitted to associate with his old friends, many of whom the regime now honours as its leading enemies. No one is sure why he is privileged – perhaps because Klenek is useful propaganda, somebody the regime can hold up to its foreign critics as an artist who lives as he wishes. Also, by letting him work abroad, they can continue to tax his large foreign earnings. And, explains Bolotka, Klenek may well be a spy. 'Probably he tells them things,' says Bolotka. 'Not that it matters. Nobody tells him anything, and he knows nobody tells him anything, and they know nobody tells him anything.'

'What's the point then?'

'With Klenek the point is to spy not on politics but on sex. The house is bugged everywhere. The secret police listen to the tape recordings of Klenek's parties. They prowl outside and look in the windows. It's their job. Sometimes they even see something and get excited. This is a pleasant distraction from the pettiness and viciousness of their regular work. It does them good. It does everybody good. Fifteen-year-old girls come to Klenek's. They dress up like streetwalkers and come from as far away as a hundred miles. Everybody, even schoolchildren, is looking for fun. You like orgies, you come with me. Since the Russians, the best orgies in Europe are in Czechoslovakia. Less liberty, better fucks. You can do whatever you want at Klenek's. No drugs, but plenty of whiskey. You can fuck, you can masturbate, you can look at dirty pictures, you can look at yourself in the mirror, you can do nothing. All the best people are there. Also the worst. We are all comrades now. Come to the orgy, Zuckerman – you will see the final stage of the revolution.'

Klenek's is a small seventeenth-century palazzo on the Kampa, a little residential island we reach by descending a long wet stairway from the Charles Bridge. Standing in the cobbled square outside of Klenek's, I hear the Vltava churning past the deep stone embankment. I've walked with Bolotka from my hotel through the maze of the ghetto, passing on the way the capsized tombstones of what he informs me is the oldest Jewish cemetery left in Europe. Within the iron grating, the jumble of crooked, eroded markers looks less like a place of eternal rest than something a cyclone has torn apart. Twelve thousand Jews buried in layers in what in New York would be a small parking lot. Drizzle dampening the tombstones, ravens in the trees.

Klenek's: large older women in dark rayon raincoats, young pretty women with jewels and long dresses, stout middle-aged men dressed in boxy suits and looking like postal clerks, elderly men with white hair, a few slight young men in American jeans – but no fifteen-year-old girls.

Bolotka may be having some fun exaggerating for his visitor the depths of Prague depravity – a little cold water on free-world fantasies of virtuous political suffering.

Beside me on a sofa, Bolotka explains who is who and who likes what.

'That one was a journalist till they fired him. He loves pornography. I saw him with my eyes fucking a girl from behind and reading a dirty book at the same time. That one, he is a terrible abstract painter. The best abstract painting he did was the day the Russians came. He went out and painted over all the street signs so the tanks wouldn't know where they were. He has the longest prick in Prague. That one, the little clerk, that is Mr Vodicka. He is a very good writer, an excellent writer, but everything scares him. If he sees a petition, he passes out. When you bring him to life again, he says he will sign it: he has ninety-eight per cent reason to sign, and only two per cent reason not to sign, and he has only to think about the two per cent and he will sign. By the next day the two per cent has grown to one hundred per cent. Just this week Mr Vodicka told the government that if he made bad politics he is sorry. He is hoping this way they will let him write again about his perversion.'

'Will they?'

'Of course not. They will tell him now to write a historical novel about Pilsen beer.'

We are joined by a tall, slender woman, distinguished by a mass of hair dyed the colour of a new penny and twisted down over her forehead in curls. Heavy white makeup encases her sharp, birdlike face. Her eyes are grey cat-eyes, her smile is beckoning. 'I know who you are,' she whispers to me.

'And you are who?'

'I don't know. I don't even feel I exist.' To Bolotka: 'Do I exist?'

'This one is Olga,' Bolotka says. 'She has the best legs in Prague. She is showing them to you. Otherwise she does not exist.'

Mr Vodicka approaches Olga, bows like a courtier, and takes – her hand. He is a little, unobtrusive man of sixty, neatly dressed and wearing heavy spectacles. Olga pays him no attention.

'My lover wants to kill me,' she says to me.

Mr Vodicka is whispering in her ear. She waves him away, but passionately he presses her hand to his cheek.

'He wants to know if she has any boys for him,' Bolotka explains.

'Who is she?'

'She was the most famous woman in the country. Olga wrote our love stories. A man stood her up in a restaurant and she wrote a love story, and the whole country talked about why he stood her up. She had an abortion and she told the doctor it could be one of eleven men, and the whole country debated whether it could actually be so many. She went to bed with a woman and the whole country read the story and was guessing who it was. She was seventeen, she already wrote a bestseller, Touha. Longing. Our Olga loves most the absent thing. She loves the Bohemian countryside. She loves her childhood – But always something is missing. Olga suffers the madness that follows after loss. And this even *before* the Russians. Klenek saw her in a cafe, a tall country girl, her heart full of *touha*, and he took her here to live with him. This is over twenty years ago. For seven years Olga was married. She had a child. Poor child. Now her husband runs off with the other famous woman in our country, a beautiful Czech actress who he will destroy in America, and Olga, Klenek looks after.'

'Why does she need looking after?'

'Why do you need looking after?' Bolotka asks her.

'This is awful,' she says. 'I hear stories about myself tonight. Stories about who I fuck. I would never fuck such people.'

'Why do you need looking after, Olga?' Bolotka asks again.

'Because I'm shaking. Feel me shaking. I never stop shaking. I am frightened of everything.' Points to me. 'I am frightened of him.' She flops down onto the sofa, in the space between Bolotka and me. I feel pressing against mine the best legs in Prague. Also believe I feel the *touha*.

Sports, Fairs, Spectacles

[93] The training method of Emil Zátopek, the Czech athlete who won the gold medal for 10,000m at the 1948 Olympics in London and achieved a remarkable golden treble in the 1952 Olympics in Helsinki – 10,000m, 5,000m *and* the marathon – the only athlete to complete such a feat at one Olympiad; from *Zátopek: The Marathon Victor* by František Kožík, translated by Jean Layton, Prague, 1954.

Zátopek's method is not the only one that has been used by the world's best runners in recent times for producing outstanding results. The Swedes have invented their 'Fartleck' [*sic*] (running through playing) with which they have achieved excellent performances. Both these training methods, the Swedish and that of Zátopek, use the so-called interval method. This method consists in repeating certain distances over and over again, followed by shorter or longer intervals.

By running fairly short distances the runner makes sure of his speed. By repeating the distances over and over again he develops his power of endurance. What then is the difference between the Swedish 'Fartleck' and Zátopek's training method?

The Fartleck is entirely run in the woods, on soft moss. The speed and the length of the distance are altered according to inclination. If there is too much of one or other, then the runner makes a break. He should not wear himself out in training, so that he has sufficient reserves left for racing.

. . . In the neighbourhood of Prague there are only woods with hard, firm ground. There is no sense training in them.

. . . It would of course be ideal if Zátopek could run his training distances in the woods, on soft mossy ground. In that way he would save his legs and so he could increase his daily quota, that would increase his stamina and Zátopek would probably run even better records.

How does Zátopek carry out his method in practice?

The basis of all Zátopek's performances lies in his daily training. In wind and rain, in frost and snow, in summer and winter, the whole year through without a break. If his work takes him into the country, he runs his distances in the woods, the fields, the meadows or on the roads. If he is in town – and he is now domiciled in Prague – then he trains on the track, whatever time of the year it is. In bad weather he wears his military hobnail boots, otherwise tennis shoes or sneakers, according to the condition of the ground.

His actual training is a combination of interval runs and runs at alternating speeds.

Usually he runs 5 × 200 metres, then 20 × 400 metres and then back to 5 × 200 metres all at racing speed. However the above-mentioned distances are not independent runs, they are linked together by fast jogs of about 200 metres to form one complete whole.

[94] Martina Navrátilová begins her training in a Prague tennis club; from *Martina Unauthorized* by Adrianne Blue, London, 1994.

The Czech Republic is a tiny country. Drive two hours in any direction and you are in another land, Poland to the north, Austria if you go south, and to the west, Germany. All of these countries are many times bigger than the Republic yet only massive Germany has had as many tennis champions. It is not anything mysterious in the water. Rather, for generations tennis has been one of the big sports in the Republic and Czech bureaucrats fought hard to convince the Communist regime, which usually backed only Olympic sport, to back tennis in Czechoslovakia.

The Czech version of America's Nick Bollettieri tennis academy was of as high quality but infinitely more low key. Instead of moving in, players who were accepted for coaching came after school. This wasn't simply a matter of paying for it. For this you had to qualify and, in what was a crucial revision of the standard communist doctrine, the Czech Tennis Federation offered training to each according to ability, providing not lavishly, but well. The training programme had a bit in common with the public parks systems that existed on a smaller scale in America and gave us Wimbledon champions Althea Gibson and Billie Jean King. It is similar to the open, non-class-based system which is struggling to be born in Britain and may by the year 2000 result in champions.

To sail through the Czech system of elite clubs for elite players, however, you needed enthusiastic parents. When her stepfather promised that she would win Wimbledon one day, Martina says, 'I believed him. He didn't tell me I was going to do it nine times, though.'

To fulfil their dream, when she was nine he took her to Prague for a try out with the Czech equivalent of a tennis pro at Klamovka Tennis Club. She passed it. 'I think we can do something with her,' the instructor George Parma said.

Twice a week after school, Martina now took the train to Prague where she boarded the tram that went down busy Plzeňská street. Instead of the splendid old city of architectural fame, on the tram ride from Smíchov station Martina passed through the seedy Prague of dour reality. Streets of drab brown buildings, many with scaffolding affixed to hold them up, advertised their decades of neglect. For the older generation decrepitude became a symbol of resistance. A state of depression was fairly universal. Everyone was employed, no one worked. Everyone knew how to look busy. 'We pretend we're working,' a Czech ironist quipped, 'and they pretend they're paying us.'

The child Martina understood little of this. But she couldn't miss seeing the decrepitude. As soon as you get off the tram at the stop called Klamovka at the edge of Klamovka park, you have to cross traffic-filled Plzeňská street. Martin's other grandmother Anděla Šubertová, her father's mother, was often there waiting at the tram stop for Martina. They would cross together very carefully, the little old lady in black dress and stockings and the long, lean child. Together they would walk up the hill, past the bus stop and the big forsythia bush, to the tennis courts. Anděla Šubertová, whom Martina called Babička – the Czech word for grandmother – lived in a flat virtually in sight of the tennis club. Sometimes she stayed to watch the practice. Babička was not interested in tennis but her Martinka was her 'golden little girl'. Martina loved Babička very much. Long after she had moved to America, Martina had recurring dreams about running and trying to get to Babička, whom she couldn't reach. 'She's in my dreams,' Martina said, 'more than anybody else.'

After the mid-week session, Babička usually shepherded Martinka back to the tram, but on Friday nights she stayed over. There was a lesson on Saturday. Martinka and Babička had a wonderful time doing crosswords and eating suppers of chicken with carrot salad, which Babicka always pointed out was good for your eyes. 'People say grandparents are going out of style. I had the real thing: a little old Czech grandmother who loved me and whose memory keeps me going today.'

The Klamovka Tennis Club, which housed the first indoor courts in Prague in what looked like an aircraft hangar, is not what it has been. It is hard to find now, its light not so much hidden under a bushel as behind a billboard and a car-hire agency. Two men cleaning the interior of one car point me beyond the rental office to what looks like an empty car park. There are puddles in the cracked paving. This is all that remains of the covered tennis courts.

'Seven years ago, it fell down,' explains the grey-haired current director. As the Communists were still in power, it was not rebuilt. It just missed out on the Velvet Revolution.

The outdoor tennis courts beyond, surrounded by trees, are so near the main thoroughfare that you can hear the trams if you listen for them. You don't. Like Sparta, the more elite club Martina would move to later, it is green here, with much foliage. Calm, beautiful. The backboards and the wooden surrounds are painted the dull, dark, elegant green of England and Europe. Few American courts are painted this traditional colour. On a cold, damp afternoon, the courts are deserted, but they are well maintained, the clay intact. Even in the gloom of a rainy day, you can imagine the absent players, and almost hear the ball thunk. In this weather, there are only a few players even at the Czech showcase courts on the other side of Prague. George Parma too is long gone. Even before Martina, he went to America.

The new director, Václav Bloha, lives in the building beside the court. 'Write only nice things,' he advised, 'because she is a wonderful player and a wonderful woman.' She *is* a hero to the Czech people.

How to be Prague-matic

[95] To a true Praguer, Jerome K. Jerome believes, a window always proves too strong a temptation; from *Three Men on a Bummel*, London, 1900.

Prague is one of the most interesting towns in Europe. Its stones are saturated with history and romance; its every suburb must have been a battlefield. It is the town that conceived the Reformation and hatched the Thirty Years War. But half Prague's troubles, one imagines, might have been saved to it, had it possessed windows less large and temptingly convenient.

The first of these mighty catastrophes it set rolling by throwing the seven Catholic councillors from the windows of its New Town Hall on to the pikes of the Hussites below. Later, it gave the signal for the second by again throwing the Imperial councillors from the windows of the old Castle in Hradčany – Prague's second 'defenestration.' Since, other fateful questions have been decided in Prague, one assumes from their having been concluded without violence that such must have been discussed in cellars. The window,

as an argument, one feels, would always have proved too
strong a temptation to any true-born Praguer.

[96] On the Czechs' propensity to 'bend' before superior force; from *Utz* by Bruce Chatwin, London, 1988.

Knowing no one in Prague, I asked a friend, a historian who
specialized in the Iron Curtain countries, if there was
anyone he'd recommend me to see.

He replied that Prague was still the most mysterious of
European cities, where the supernatural was always a possibility. The Czechs' propensity to 'bend' before superior
force was not necessarily a weakness. Rather, their meta-
physical view of life encouraged them to look on acts of
force as ephemera.

'Of course,' he said, 'I could send you to any number of
intellectuals. Poets, painters, filmmakers.' Providing I could
face an interminable whine about the role of the artist in a
totalitarian state, or wished to go to a party that would end
in a partouse.

I protested. Surely he was exaggerating?

'No,' he shook his head. 'I don't think so.'

He would be the last to denigrate a man who risked the
labour camp for publishing a poem in a foreign journal.
But, in his view, the true heroes of this impossible situation
were people who wouldn't raise a murmur against the Party
or State – yet who seemed to carry the sum of Western
Civilization in their heads.

'With their silence,' he said, 'they inflict a final insult on
the State, by pretending it does not exist.' Where else would
one find, as he had, a tram-ticket salesman who was a scholar
of the Elizabethan stage? Or a street-sweeper who had
written a philosophical commentary on the Anaximander
Fragment?

He finished by observing that Marx's vision of an age of
infinite leisure had, in one sense, come true. The State, in its
efforts to wipe out 'traces of individualism', offered limit-
less time for the intelligent individual to dream his private
and heretical thoughts.

[97] After the fall of Communism, a Welsh travel writer finds that 'normality has returned' to the Czechs and their country; from *Fifty Years of Europe: An Album* by Jan Morris, London, 1997.

So normality [*had*] returned to the Czech Republic, which I first knew as part of Czechoslovakia, and which had imprinted its name and character upon the conscious-ness of all Europe since the day in 1938 when Neville Chamberlain, Prime Minister of Great Britain, fatefully described it as a faraway country of whose people 'we know nothing'. When I first went there, in the 1950s, it was a country of degraded servility, where everything seemed to smell of sausages. The slogans of Communist piety nagged from every hoarding, the drab emblems of State manage-ment were on every corner shop. The only foreigners around were approved comrades – Afghans and Syrians, come to buy arms or cars, ideologically correct delegations of Poles, Romanians, Hungarians and East Germans, or groups of square-shouldered Russians in baggy trousers and drab hats.

At that time I took note, for literary purposes, of an apart-ment block at the corner of Kaprova and Valentinská streets in Prague. A cross between baroque and art nouveau, it had a small onion dome on one corner, and was embellished all over with symbolic images. There were balconies, and window-boxes, and lace curtains in the windows. A tobacco shop stood on the ground floor, and at the end of the street, over the river, you could see the spires and battlements of Hradčany, the old stronghold of the Czech kings. I chose to describe this building as an allegorical hostel of Communism, and fancied it full of drabness, fear, longing, austerity, com-pulsory pictures of Lenin and nosy-parker informants. I saw it too swirled about, there at the road junction, by the whole parade of European history. I saw the armies of Franz Josef, Adolf Hitler and Joseph Stalin all marching past its doors. I saw ecstatically courageous students shouting slogans and waving banners. Commissioners, gauleiters and commissars drove officiously by. Franz Kafka's faceless functionaries trudged past on their way to the interrogation rooms, Jaroslav Hašek's Good Soldier Švejk, bless his heart, smiled ironically down on the lot of them.

But years later I went back to the corner of Kaprova and Valentinská streets to reimagine these matters, and this time I saw something quite new on an upper balcony of the apartment block, above the potted geraniums. It was a TV satellite dish, the universal emblem of market-force society. It suggested to me the olive leaf that the dove brought back to Noah, when the flood began to recede.

Had history ended in the Czech Republic? Going back to the country a few years after the Velvet Revolution which finally got rid of the Communists, sometimes I felt it had: the one great thing that had happened since was the voluntary separation of Slovakia from Czechoslovakia, and that had been scarcely noticed by the world at large (although, by an irony worthy of Švejk himself, it was the very separation which, when Hitler implicitly decreed it, gave rise to the Second World War). In the 1950s Prague had seemed to me the most oppressive of the Communist capitals of eastern Europe, but its fate was tragic and tremendous. Forty years on, the collapse of the Soviet Empire had left its own smouldering layers of sleaze and squalor, but the public miseries of the place were miseries familiar to us all. Stalinist Prague was sufficiently corrupt, God knows, but in institutional ways: at least in the 1950s one was not cheated by taxi-drivers or robbed by jostling pickpockets. The secret policemen were everywhere in those awful old times, every official was waiting to be bribed, but there were none of the beggars sitting with bowed heads, sometimes with their eyes hopelessly closed, who represented contemporary sadness in the 1990s.

In 1993 I went to a political meeting in Old Town Square, scene of heroic demonstrations in the days of the oppression, to hear a speaker inveighing against Germans, Gypsies, prostitutes and illegal immigrants; he was supported by skinheads and miscellaneous layabouts, protected by mounted police, assaulted by flying bottles and the odd rotten vegetable. Prague had joined the ordinary world, and history was at least on the blink. In 1957 I had been warned, by somebody who knew, that not only my room in the morose Palace Hotel but actually my table in its restaurant was likely to be bugged. Now the same hotel offered American cable television in its bedrooms, a lavish variety of soaps, lotions, bath salts and shower-caps, and such excellent little notepads beside its telephones that I helped myself to a few from the maid's trolley in the corridor. When the Czech journalist Karel Kyncl returned to Prague in 1989, after seven years of exile, he said it was like sleep-walking.

[98] 'The Royal Pavilion' – a poem by Jaroslav Seifert, the 1984 Czech Nobel Prize winner for Literature, translated by Ewald Ossers.

> Whenever I gaze out on Prague
> – and I do so constantly and always with bated breath
> because I love her –
> I turn my mind to God
> wherever he may hide from me,
> beyond the starry mists
> or just behind that moth-eaten screen,
> to thank him
> for granting me that magnificent setting
> to live in.
> I love her fire-charred walls
> to which we clung during the war
> so as to hold out.
> I would not change them for anything in the world.
> Not even for others,
> not even if the Eiffel Tower rose between them
> and the Seine flowed sadly past,
> not even for all the gardens of paradise
> full of flowers.
>
> When I shall die – and this will be quite soon –
> I shall carry in my heart
> this city's destiny.

Bibliography

ANDERSEN, HANS CHRISTIAN, *Poet's Bazaar*, trans. Charles Beckwith, London, 1846.

APPOLINAIRE, GUILLAUME, *Le Paesant de Prague*, trans. Pascal Thivillon, Paris, 1967.

BAKER, JAMES, *Pictures from Bohemia*, London, 1897.

BAUER, JOHANN, *Kafka and Prague*, trans. P. S. Falla, London, 1971.

BETTS, REGINALD ROBERT, *Essays in Czech History*, London, 1969.

BLUE, ADRIANNE, *Martina Unauthorised*, London, 1994.

BRAUN, GEORG and FRANZ HOGENBERG, *Civitates Orbis Terrarum*, 1602.

BROD, MAX, *The Biography of Franz Kafka*, trans. G. Humphreys Roberts, London, 1947.

BROOKS, STEPHEN, *The Double Eagle*, London, 1988.

BRUCE LOCKHART, ROBERT H., *Retreat from Glory*, London, 1934.

—, *The Diaries of Sir Robert Bruce Lockhart*, London, 1980.

CAMUS, ALBERT, *Diaries*, Paris, 1965, trans. Pascal Thivillon.

ČAPEK, KAREL, *Talks with T. G. Masaryk*, Connecticut, 1995.

CARLYLE, THOMAS, *History of Friedrich II of Prussia called Frederick the Great*, London, 1858–1865.

CHATWIN, BRUCE, *Utz*, London, 1988.

CLAVERIE, JANA and ALENA KOUBOVÁ, *Prague*, Paris, 2002.

COWLES, VIRGINIA, *Looking for Trouble*, London, 1942.

DAUBENY, PETER, *My World of Theatre*, London, 1971.

DAVENPORT, MARCIA, *The Valley of Decision*, London, 1946.

DEACON, RICHARD, *John Dee*, London, 1968.

DEIGHTON, LEN, *Funeral in Berlin*, London, 1965.

DENIS, ERNEST, *Prague*, ed. H. Hantich, Prague, 1902.

DRACULIĆ, SLAVENKA, *How We Survived Communism And Even Laughed*, London, 1987.

ELIOT, GEORGE, *The Journals of George Eliot*, ed. M. Harris and J. Johnson, London, 1998.

FEINSTEIN, ADAM, *Pablo Neruda: A Passion for Life*, London, 2004.

FERMOR, PATRICK LEIGH, *A Time of Gifts*, London, 1977.

FORMAN, MILOŠ and JAN NOVÁK, *Turnaround*, London, 1994.

GEORGE, G.J., *They Betrayed Czechoslovakia*, London, 1938.

HAVEL, VÁCLAV, *Disturbing the Peace*, New York, 1990.

HIBBERT, CHRISTOPHER, *Nelson: A Personal History*, London, 1994.

HRABAL, BOHUMIL, *The Pink Scarf*, trans. James Naughton, London, 1995.

IVANOV, MIROSLAV, *The Assassination of Heydrich*, London, 1973.

JANOUCH, GUSTAV, *Conversations with Kafka*, trans. Goronwy Rees, London, 1971.

JEROME, K(LAPKA) JEROME, *Three Men on a Bummel*, London, 1900.

JIRÁSEK, ALOIS, *The Old Czech Legends*, trans. Edith Pargeter, Prague, 1963.

KENNAN, GEORGE, F., *Memoirs: 1925–1950*, Boston, 1967.

KLÍMA, IVAN, *The Spirit of Prague*, London, 1994.

KOŽÍK, FRANTIŠEK, *Zátopek: The Marathon Victor*, trans. Jean Layton, Prague, 1954.

KUNES, KAREN VON, *Beyond the Imaginable*, Prague, 1999.

LAMARR, HEDY, *Ecstasy And Me*, London, 1966.

LARGE, BRIAN, *Smetana*, London, 1970.

LÚTZOW, FRANCIS, *A History of Bohemian Literature*, London, 1937.

MARGOLIUS KOVÁLY, HEDA, *I Don't Want To Remember*, London, 1973.

MAYRINK, GUSTAV, *The Angel of the West Window*, London, 1991.

MORRIS, JAN, *Fifty Years of Europe: An Album*, London, 1997.

MORYSON, FYNES, *An Itinerary*, London, 1907–1908.

MOZART, W. A., *Letters*, trans. Emily Anderson, London, 1990.

NERUDA, JAN, *What Shall We Do With It?*, trans. Michael Henry Heim, Prague, 1995.

PARROT, SIR CECIL, *The Serpent and The Nightingale*, London, 1977.

PATIN, CHARLES, *Travels thro' Germany, Bohemia, Swisserland, Holland and other Parts of Europe*, London, 1697.

PECH, STANLEY Z., *The Czech Revolution of 1848*, The University of North Carolina, Chapel Hill, 1969.

PETIŠKA, EDUARD, *A Treasury of Tales from the Kingdom of Bohemia*, Prague, 1994.

—, *The Golem*, Prague, 1994.

—, *The Lives of St Wenceslas, St Ludmila and St Adalbert*, Prague, 1994.

PIOZZI, HARRIET LYNCH, *Observations and Reflections*, London, 1789.

RIPELLINO, ANGELO MARIA, *Magic Prague*, trans. David Newton Marinelli, London, 1994.

RODIN, AUGUSTE, *His Letters*, Paris, 1902.

ROTH, PHILLIP, *The Prague Orgy*, London, 1985.

SEIFERT, JAROSLAV, *The Royal Pavilion*, trans. Ewald Ossers, London, 1989.

SHERRY, NORMAN, *The Life of Graham Greene, Volume Two: 1939–1955*, London, 1994.

WATSON, FRANCIS, *Wallenstein*, London, 1938.

WILSON, DAVID ALEC, *Carlyle*, London, 1929.

Index

The *Traveller's Companions*

The *Traveller's Companions* series was born out of the need to provide information for tourists whose imaginations and interest needed to be stimulated and amused by quality material that went beyond the standard travel guide.

The guiding principles for selecting material were (a) a master list of places to visit; (b) the most exciting historical events that happened in each place; and (c) the most colourful and vivid descriptions of those events.

A lot of research is required in the production of each title but the result, I hope, is a series of timeless companions to exhilarating cities.

Laurence Kelly, *Series Editor*

Praise for the series

'Nothing less than a masterpiece . . . the perfect companion for the intending traveller, bringing the city's every aspect vividly alive'
Sunday Times (*A Traveller's Companion to St Petersburg*)

'A brilliant historical anthology . . . which I read from cover to cover, relishing the author's witty selection of writings.'
Spectator (*A Traveller's Companion to Venice*)

'The best conceivable companion guide to the city.'
Country Life (*A Traveller's Companion to Florence*)

To order further *Traveller's Companions*

No. of copies	Title	Price (incl. p&p)	Total
	Dublin	£9.99	
	Edinburgh	£9.99	
	Florence	£9.99	
	Istanbul	£9.99	
	London	£12.99	
	Madrid	£9.99	
	Moscow	£9.99	
	St Petersburg	£9.99	
	Venice	£9.99	
	Grand Total		**£**

Name: _____

Address: _____

_____ Postcode: _____

Daytime Tel. No. / Email _____
(in case of query)

Three ways to pay:

1. **For express service telephone the TBS order line on 01206 255 800 and quote 'CRBK'. Order lines are open Monday–Friday 8:30a.m. – 5:30p.m.**

2. I enclose a cheque made payable to **TBS Ltd** for £_____

3. Please charge my ❑ Visa ❑ Mastercard ❑ Amex ❑ Switch (switch issue no. ....) £_____

   Card number: _____

   Expiry date: _____ Signature _____
   (your signature is essential when paying by credit card)

Please return forms (*no stamp required*) to, Constable & Robinson Ltd, FREEPOST NAT6619, 3 The Lanchesters, 162 Fulham Palace Road, London W6 9ER. All books subject to availability.

Enquiries to readers@constablerobinson.com
www.constablerobinson.com

Constable & Robinson Ltd (directly or via its agents) may mail or phone you about promotions or products. Tick box if you do not want these from us ❑ or our subsidiaries.